Presented to:

_____

From:

_____

Date:

_____

THE TURQUOISE TABLE

FINDING COMMUNITY AND CONNECTION IN YOUR OWN FRONT YARD

Kristin Schell

THOMAS NELSON
Since 1798

Published in Nashville, Tennessee, by Thomas Nelson. Thomas Nelson is a registered trademark of HarperCollins Christian Publishing, Inc.

Thomas Nelson titles may be purchased in bulk for educational, business, fund-raising, or sales promotional use. For information, please e-mail SpecialMarkets@ThomasNelson.com.

ISBN-13: 978-0-7180-9558-1

Printed in the United States of America

17 18 19 20 21 LSC 8 7 6 5 4 3

For Tony—the love of my life and head of our table.

Will, Anna, Ellie, and Sarah—may you find your
place in this world, with eyes on the next, set
tables of your own, and remember you are always
welcome to return to the place called home.

CONTENTS

1

To Gather
Around a Table

> A single conversation across the
> table with a wise man is better than
> ten years mere study of books.
>
> *Henry Wadsworth Longfellow*

My love affair with the table began with an F in high school French class. The failing grade prompted my parents to send me on an overseas immersion experience in France, where open-air food markets, home-cooked meals with host families, and quaint bistros opened a new way of experiencing the importance of gathering around tables to share meals and life.

That summer I learned far more than how to conjugate verbs. The most powerful experience wasn't the language or the scrumptious new foods like chocolate éclairs and croque monsieurs . . . it

was the ritual of sitting at the table. People in France gathered at tables not just once a week, not just for holidays, but three times a day, giving a whole new meaning to "leisurely meal."

Their lunch lasted two hours; dinner could last all night. One night dinner with my host family was still going strong at 10:00 p.m. Gregarious in story, the father slammed his fists down on the table, the water carafe spilling over. The conversation was exuberant, although the details were lost on me, as I still hadn't mastered the language. Their heads were thrown back in laughter, and the entire family was engaged. I didn't need to understand the conversation to know I craved this kind of experience at the dinner table. My French brother, Phillipe, slapped my shoulder in a gesture for me to join in. I belonged at the table.

While I savored Brie and baguettes in the tiny French village of Ornans, I thought of our table back home. Adjacent to the kitchen, the dining room featured a modern, custom-made Lucite table with navy blue velvet, high-back chairs. The fabulously stylish clear table, however, was only used for special occasions such as Christmas, Easter, and dinner parties.

Sitting at the simple table in France I noticed the contrast immediately and craved the slower, authentic time to connect. I was a stranger in a foreign land, yet being at the table in France fed a basic need—a need every human shares—to belong. The experience at the table was more than a meal; it was nourishment for my soul.

France offered me a model of what *could be*.

LONGING FOR THE TABLE

Two decades later, as a busy wife and mom in a suburban neighborhood in Texas, I realized again how crazy life is and how laughable the vision of a long lunch seemed. I didn't realize you can't import a cultural value as easily as a jar of Nutella; and I struggled against a busy, hectic culture as I tried to create space to gather around my own table for laughter and conversation. Most days it was a challenge to get the Crock-Pot plugged in, much less to get my busy family of six to slow down and sit down at the table.

It gave me a pit in my stomach. Our four children were growing up in an era where handwritten letters and talking on the telephone were as foreign to them as those first few days in France were to me. They were beginning to use emojis and photos instead of proper sentences to communicate with their friends and each other. I was afraid to ask the question aloud, "Are we losing the ability to sit at the table and talk?" Forget learning a new language, I feared we were losing the art of conversation.

I wanted to recreate something rich and real again—like what I experienced all those years ago in France.

And having friends over felt impossible! Trying to coordinate schedules between work and volunteer commitments, school meetings, soccer practice, and band concerts was futile. All these were good activities—but they left little or no time to sit down and catch up.

There we all were, calendars beeping notifications while we texted our apologies to each other, waving a quick hello in the carpool lane. This isn't how it's supposed to be, is it? I wanted to recreate something rich and real again—like what I experienced all those years ago in France. I wanted the family table experience, and I wanted to extend it to other important people in my life. So I tried. I tried hard.

Because my brain was already on overdrive, I consulted Pinterest and flipped through *Bon Appétit*, *Better Homes & Gardens*, and other glossy magazines for recipes and decoration ideas. I over-complicated everything and wore myself out. Instead of slowing down for a leisurely time with friends and family, I was busier than ever. The more I talked with people, the more I realized we all struggle with being too busy. We are living frazzled lifestyles, disconnected from authentic friendships in a society that idolizes busyness. It's taking its toll.

Somewhere along the way, exhausted and discouraged and coming unhinged, I scored another big fat F. Once again I was failing. This time I was trying too hard, focusing on the wrong things, worried about the food and the perfection of hosting people for parties. My effort to recreate the magic of gathering at the table bombed like a fallen soufflé.

I struggled to find my way back to a table that would welcome people with ease and create a sense of belonging. I cried. I prayed. I just couldn't see what to do, until one day, it appeared:

the Turquoise Table. It literally landed in my front yard—an ordinary wooden picnic table that sparked a new way of seeing what belonging could look like. It didn't look quite like the tables in France, but it captured the essence of belonging as curious friends and neighbors stepped out to find out what this table was about, and they sat down to find out it was for them.

The Turquoise Table brought with it far more than I ever imagined. It led to a revival of community in the simplest place of all: a table in our front yard.

I'll tell you the story of the Turquoise Table and how it's led to a movement of Front Yard People—people just like you and me who want to create community right where they live. It's a story that flows from my experience as a Christian, and at the same time you'll see this table is not about a special person or a particular faith. The Turquoise Table is a place for everyone from every walk of life to sit down in safety, dignity, respect, and love—to be heard and to belong.

If you are busy and overwhelmed, the last thing you need is one more project, one more thing to do. Well, you'll see the Turquoise Table offers simplicity. It's more than a table; it's a symbol of reaching out and making room without all the fuss and frenzy.

In the following pages I offer simple ideas and tips so you can begin using the Turquoise Table in your community and provide solutions to questions you may have. I'll share stories from real people who are using their tables every day, all year long, to enjoy old friends and make new ones. You will see how uncomplicated life at the table can be.

Sometimes we are called far and wide on a mission, but more often we are called to love others in our everyday, ordinary lives . . . right where we live: in our own front yards.

This book is my invitation to you. An invitation to join me at the Turquoise Table and to live as Front Yard People. Come to the table, friends.

Kristin Schell

2

FRAZZLED
AND DISTRACTED

If there is room in the heart,
there is room in the house.

Danish Proverb

Ten years ago I sat next to my husband, Tony, in the conference room of a title company signing a gazillion papers to purchase our home. The original homeowner sat across from us. Near the end of our document-signing marathon, she made a plea.

"We have a tradition in the neighborhood—an annual Memorial Day party." She began sharing stories about the "Party in the Cove," named for the cul-de-sac where our new-to-us home was located. "Promise me you'll keep the Cove parties going for the neighborhood."

I had no idea what I was promising, but a party sounded easy enough, and fun. "Of course," I said without much thought. Never mind that I didn't know anyone on our new street. Besides, it was February. I had plenty of time to figure it out.

We moved into our house, and I kept the promise to keep the Memorial Day tradition that had been going on for decades. The first year, we sent our young children door-to-door with handmade flyers touting barbecues and balloons. The Party in the Cove was such fun we continued the tradition in the years that followed. Each year the Cove party took on a different theme—we'd bring in magicians or bouncy houses, music and giant inflatable water slides. Spectacular events, these parties were loads of fun, luring everyone outside to relax and interact. They met a deeply felt need to connect, outside, where none of us had to worry about vacuuming our living room carpets or whipping up hors d'oeuvres. The party freed us from entertaining and invited us out into our yards. Though it was a huge effort for the organizers, our neighbors enjoyed the event and experienced a true sense of community.

We felt something special, together, but as soon as the

Take every opportunity to open your life and home to others. (Romans 12:13)

coolers were emptied and the lawn chairs were packed away, we disappeared behind our fences, settling into the comfort of our backyards. Twelve months is a long time to go between neighborhood get-togethers. And it's embarrassing to admit, but even after several Cove parties I didn't know for sure if it was the Gerries or the Whitneys who lived in the house with the yellow shutters three doors down. What would it take for us to gather more frequently? Couldn't we do it without bouncy houses? Could we keep it simple?

About that time, I read a Bible verse that stuck with me and kept replaying in my head: "Take every opportunity to open your life and home to others" (Romans 12:13).

WHEN HOSPITALITY FEELS HARD

The part about opening your life and home to others I had heard—so much so that it started to sound a little like a Hallmark card. But the part that kept rolling around in my head was "every opportunity." *Every* opportunity. That's a lot! That sounds like *always and constantly*! What on earth? How in the world do you do that? Not just on Thursdays if the floors are clean and the laundry is put away. Not just on Tuesdays if you're having a good hair day

Make a list of backyard activities you and your family enjoy.

_____

_____

_____

What events or gatherings already happen in your
neighborhood?

_____

_____

_____

What aspect of hospitality feels hard for you? What holds
you back?

_____

_____

_____

and the kids are at school. Not just when you wake up and you're in the mood. But *every opportunity.*

I wanted to take Romans 12:13 to heart. I wanted to live it out in practical ways, but I was in the middle of raising and growing our family. During this time we welcomed our fourth baby, Sarah, into the world. As life was growing busier and busier, it became harder to imagine where those "every opportunities" were going to come from. I was trying hard to find ways to open my life and my home to others, both with neighbors and friends.

Beware the barrenness of a busy life.

Socrates

Over the years, I did what I thought the verse meant and managed to host parties, Bible studies, book clubs, and swim parties, but it was nuts. I was in survival mode, barely handling the carpool, and here I was trying to open my life and home at every opportunity; going wide, but not deep. I was craving depth but skimming the surface. In reality I was barely treading water, using up what little energy I had planning a play date. Clearly I was missing something about what Romans 12:13 really means.

Our kids' activities ramped up the older they got, and I kept trying to stack on another idea to open my home. It got to the point where I decided to slap a bumper sticker on the minivan that reads "Queen of Crazy." Most weeks I was wearing the cliché "It's all good!" like a cheap T-shirt. I only had time for so much and found myself screaming out to God in surrender, "Lord, edit my life!" If there was any silver lining to this craziness, it's that I wasn't alone. My friends were feeling frazzled too.

Our communication styles shifted as well. When our oldest son, Will, was born, there was no such thing as texts. But with the introduction of smart phones, we began texting instead of talking. Virtual communities were a quick and easy way to stay in touch on the go. Face-to-face conversations were often limited to the dairy aisle at the grocery store. We'd always say, "I'm fine," knowing there was more behind the pat response, but we had no time to stop and listen. We had to grab the milk and move on to the next thing.

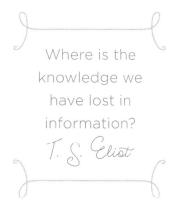

Where is the knowledge we have lost in information?

T. S. Eliot

Our culture idolizes busyness, and without knowing it, we'd fallen prey to a false sense of connection. And we continued to sit in the driver's seat of our minivans, scratching our heads, wondering, *Is this it?*

How Frazzled Are You?

CALENDAR QUIZ

Do you rule your calendar, or does your calendar rule you? Take this quiz to see how you're spending your time and energy.

Looking at my calendar stresses
me out—there's no empty space! _____ Yes _____ No

I enjoy getting together with friends,
but when I look at the calendar, the first
available date is over a month out. _____ Yes _____ No

I have a hard time saying no and
end up overcommitting myself. _____ Yes _____ No

No matter what I do, it seems every
minute of the day is scheduled
for something. _____ Yes _____ No

I often wish I had more time
for things I enjoy. _____ Yes _____ No

Everything on my calendar is
good and important. _____ Yes _____ No

I feel powerless over my time
and commitments. _____ Yes _____ No

Someone important to me has said,
"You've got too much on your plate." _____ Yes _____ No

I've missed important events because
I'm too exhausted to add one more
thing to the calendar. _____ Yes _____ No

My calendar is filled with activities and
obligations for the people I love—spouse,
children, parents. _____ Yes _____ No

Give yourself 1 point for each "yes" response.

HOW'D YOU DO?

7–10 Welcome to the Frazzled Club. It's time to slow down
         and make space for yourself.

4–6 Looks like you are managing, but guard the space you
         have created for yourself or it will fill up fast!

0–3 Well done! Looks like you are doing great finding time
         to connect. Why not encourage others by sharing your
         secret with the rest of us? Permission to slow down
         and connect might be exactly what your friends and
         neighbors need.

CRAVING COMMUNITY

We live in the digital age—the most connected era in all of history—yet statistics show we're lonelier than ever. We live in a chatty world, but we have lost the power to communicate. We're starving for connection that can't be found in a tweet or text, but only face-to-face in community.

Maybe the antidote to the frazzled lifestyle was rooted in that promise I made to continue our Party in the Cove. Maybe we needed to slow down long enough to step outside in the fresh air where our kids could run free, like we did once a year. That gathering offered hints of nostalgia, of a time before cell phones, before calendars ruled the world, when people gathered in front yards, hanging out and doing life together. It's as if the generation before us knew something we have forgotten about opening up their lives and homes to others through the simplicity of their front porch, a carefree lifestyle, being neighbors to neighbors. I felt the longing, but I was too busy spinning my wheels to open my front door and walk out onto the lawn. What would it take to reclaim community in a simple and authentic way? I wanted more for my family and our neighborhood, but I couldn't see how to fix it. Maybe you've felt this way too.

FRAZZLED AND DISTRACTED

A Turquoise Table Story

I don't remember the exact words I spoke as my children arrived sleepily in the kitchen hoping for something warm to eat for breakfast. Busy with an e-mail, I was already distracted at 6:30 a.m. I waved them away and muttered something to the tune of, "Get your own breakfast."

Seriously? I had no more than thirty minutes with the kids before they headed out the door to school, and *this* was how I greeted them? I didn't even make eye contact.

My children didn't give two flips about what kind of breakfast I served (as long as there was no visible spinach). They were just sleepy, hungry, and wanted some help getting food. Actually, what they wanted was *me*. But before the sun even lit the sky, I had already been about as inhospitable as I could be.

After the busyness of our morning routine and alone in our quiet house, I took a minute, sulking in shame, to think about what I could have done differently. For me, it hinged on one word—*distraction*. I've long forgotten the content of that 6:30

a.m. e-mail, but I'll never forget the feeling of distancing my own children. The experience served as a wakeup call.

I'd been distracted by my phone many mornings as well, checking my Instagram stream and scrolling through Facebook. Who's even on Instagram at seven in the morning? Who even cares?

I wanted to take a few minutes to turn toward our children, to give them my time, my attention. Whether I poured cereal, tossed a bagel in the toaster, or we worked together making sandwiches for school lunches, it was about being present.

Something had to change.

That afternoon I set a basket on the entry hall table for cell phones—the iBasket. Mine was the first one in. For a while I was really good about putting all our devices there, allowing *all* of us the opportunity to unplug and be present during meals and family time. For a long time I didn't check the phone until after the children left the house for school. I eliminated the phone from my morning routine and freed up space in my life, allowing me the opportunity to be their mom, sending them off with assurances they are seen and loved.

The basket has been empty lately. Feeling like I've fallen back into a default mode of distraction, it's time to bring back the iBasket to collect all our iDevices during family meals at the table. Because I never want to wave away our children. I want to look them in the eyes. Make a real connection.

With France and the nostalgia of the table always on my mind, some mornings I treat my kids to something special (that is easy for me to prepare the night before). I serve Overnight French Toast for breakfast. And I sit across from them as they eat, savoring the moment.

> ## iPhones iSolate:
>
> I've never seen a place setting—formal or casual—that includes a place for iPhones. I'm not huge on ultimatums, but this is a hill I will die on: technology is the only unwelcome guest at the table.

Overnight French Toast

1 tablespoon butter, room temperature

12 1-inch slices French "baguette-style" bread

6 large eggs

1 ¹/₂ cups milk

¹/₄ cup sugar

2 tablespoons maple syrup

2 teaspoons vanilla extract

Pinch of salt

Grease the bottom and sides of a 9 x 12-inch baking pan with butter. Arrange bread slices in the pan. In a bowl beat eggs, milk, sugar, syrup, vanilla, and salt. Pour the mixture over the bread. Turn bread slices to coat. Cover with foil or plastic wrap and refrigerate overnight.

The next morning preheat oven to 375 degrees.

Bake French toast uncovered for 15 minutes. Turn bread slices over and continue baking until golden brown, about 10 minutes.

Serve with maple syrup or jam and fresh berries.

3

You Can't Be What You Can't See

Walking with a friend in the dark is
better than walking alone in the light.

Helen Keller

uring that frazzled time of life, I managed to squeeze
in a conference in my hometown of Austin, Texas. I
was drawn to the Verge Conference for people living
out the gospel in community, which was exactly what I was longing
to do. The Austin Music Hall was jam-packed. Each speaker took
the stage for fifteen minutes. The lights went up; they gave their
talk. The music started; the lights went down. The routine was
fast, like a Twitter stream, pouring out information on discipleship
in fifteen-minute chunks.

Then the dark stage lit up, shining on Jo Saxton, a respected leader who speaks on helping people see better how to live in community with one another. She wooed me with her British accent, delivering the line that changed everything:

*"You can't *be* what you can't *see*."*

Jo said it over and over. Or maybe she only said it once, but I heard it over and over. "You can't *be* what you can't *see*." Her speech ended, the lights went down, and I sat in that dark auditorium, alone in the crowd.

I actually clenched my fists and raised them, duking it out with God while I cried in the dark. As loud music played, I pleaded with God. "I can't see how to open up my life and home to others! I can't see how to build community! I can't see how to love my neighbors! I can't *be* what I can't *see*, so *show me*!"

Right there, in the middle of the Austin Music Hall, surrounded by 1,200 people, I had a major spiritual meltdown. Then, on massive screens flanking the stage, a documentary started. The film shows an elderly woman walking slowly down cobblestone streets. She enters a food market. The subtitle says, "Ludmilla's Story."

As I watched the film, I "met" Ludmilla, an eighty-four-year-old widow in Prague. She's survived two totalitarian regimes and lives in the heart of the most atheistic country in Europe. Yet she placed a small bronze plaque on the outside of her tiny brownstone apartment that reads "Embassy of the Kingdom of Heaven."

THE MINISTRY OF PRESENCE

Every day Ludmilla opens her home to friends and strangers who need to talk. Sometimes she knows the people who come. Sometimes strangers show up—led by word of mouth. She offers them something small, nothing overdone or extravagant. Tea. A cookie from a tin. A warm, simple gesture of welcome to her table. In a way that is quiet and genuine, Ludmilla listens and prays, and

in doing so communicates that her guests matter. At her table, they belong.

Fully present, Ludmilla serves more than just cookies and tea. She offers her heart.

God answered my prayer to see how to love my neighbors with the story of a woman half the world away who was being the hands and feet of Christ. Her actions were so simple—the antithesis of the frazzled lifestyle I was living. Ludmilla modeled how simple hospitality could be through her ministry of being present. I could see it. Maybe now I could *be* it.

What would it take for *me* to put a plaque on my door that reads "Embassy of the Kingdom of Heaven"?

I'm still the same old me. The person who makes things harder than need be, planning too much, focused on the outcome, trapped in the minutiae of the doing rather than loosening my tight grip on control and resting in the being. But I was beginning to see the vast difference between entertainment and hospitality.

I needed a change of heart. Am I fully present? Are my motives for hosting self-serving or genuinely out of care, concern, and love? Am I more concerned with Kristin or with being an ambassador to the kingdom?

I really want to be like Ludmilla. Actually, I want to be a guest at her table! She's a beautiful role model of hospitality. I want to have a simple table spread with abundant love. To offer an atmosphere of joy and peace.

A CHANGE OF HEART

As my heart began to change, pieces of my life started to feel as if they had purpose. Maybe the summer in France with the longing for the table, my new home, and my promise to keep the tradition of neighborhood community going could be melded with the vision of this woman a million miles away to create the kind of inspired hospitality I could live out.

The realization hit me: I'd been making it so hard, spinning around on a hamster wheel instead of sitting still, like Ludmilla, focusing on being present. I was *doing* instead of *being,* trying hard to execute community, and it seemed so contrived. Ludmilla pointed back to the promise, to the party. Ludmilla took me back to that

If we have no peace, it is because we have forgotten we belong to each other.
Mother Teresa

table in France and its comfortable, leisurely interaction. The Party at the Cove and Ludmilla's presence were beginning to show me how gathering people at a table can help them belong.

But what could I do in a suburban neighborhood in Texas that would offer the same experience Ludmilla was providing in her tiny Prague apartment? I don't have the time Ludmilla does to be available to people throughout the day, so I knew whatever I did would look different. But I could feel my heart shifting from confusion to possibilities. I still didn't have the precise answer, but hope was born.

Let's get real. Neither you nor I have very much in common with an eighty-four-year-old woman in Prague. But that doesn't let us off the hook. Romans 12:13 remains the same no matter where you live or what stage of life you're in. You might live in a gated community, apartment complex, rural area, city, or suburb. Maybe you're single or a grandmother or a mother of eight. Whatever your situation, how can you be present for others? What simple ways can you let people know they matter and create space for people to belong?

Ludmilla took every opportunity to open her home and life to others. It wasn't hard. She didn't consult Pinterest. She wasn't frazzled. She was simply open to the people who came to her, making them feel they belonged, right where she lived.

I could feel I was on the verge of doing this too, but God knew I needed one more little push. He gave me a dare.

In the book *A Meal with Jesus* by Tim Chester, I read this quote and knew God was speaking to me:

> Don't start with a big program . . . Start personally and start in your home.
>
> I dare you.
>
> I dare you in the name of Jesus Christ . . .
>
> Begin by opening your home for community . . .
>
> All you have to do is open your home and begin.
>
> FRANCIS SCHAEFFER, THEOLOGIAN AND
> FOUNDER OF L'ABRI COMMUNITY

A dare? I'm from Texas, where a double-dog dare is hard to resist. But a dare in the name of Jesus . . . it made me squirmy, like it might be sacrilegious. But God knew my longing to create space for people to belong. I accepted that dare. With God's help, I took the dare and prayed, "Here I am, God. Give me eyes to see."

Love Where You Live

Grab a pencil and a piece of paper. These questions will help you think about what makes your community unique.

1. Make a list of neighbors you know by name and the ones you don't. For the ones you don't know, write something like "the man in the brick house two doors down."
2. What's special about your neighborhood?
3. What's your favorite thing about your community?
4. If you could change something about where you live, what would it be?
5. Outside of your home and neighborhood, where do you spend the most time? Work, carpool, school, etc., are possibilities.
6. What is your favorite way to gather with your friends?
7. What food reminds you of home? What's your favorite comfort food?
8. In what ways has God gifted or equipped you? (Organizing, being an extrovert, cooking, etc.)
9. If time, money, or your job weren't issues to consider, what would you do to create community?

Now that you know yourself and your community better, start thinking about where you could possibly incorporate the Turquoise Table where people can gather. If you now realize you spend more time at work, maybe that's where you can think about gathering people.

A Turquoise Table Story

"Are you sure it's not going to be a problem?" I could almost hear my friend's teeth gritting through the phone as she desperately hoped I would agree.

"Of course not. Truly, it's not that big of a deal." I only half believed hosting a party in my backyard on such short notice would be fine. "Let me talk to Tony and firm up a few details, but we're good."

I hung up the phone and raced through the house to find my husband reclined in his zero-gravity chair working methodically on a spreadsheet.

"So, that party I'm hosting on Sunday with Susie? We need to move it here. The plumbing's delayed on their lake house renovations and won't be ready in time."

"That's fine."

I was surprised he was that accommodating, as Tony is an extreme introvert who often disappears in the middle of a party to retreat to his room—a challenge for me, given my gift of hospitality and willingness to take the dare to open my life and our home to others.

I gestured to our patio. "Honey, in case you haven't noticed, we have no backyard furniture. Zilch. *Nada*. Except those cheap chairs from two summers ago."

"There's nothing wrong with those chairs."

"They're hideous! But that's not the point. I need help. We are having a party here, and I have no place for people to sit and eat barbecue."

"What kind of barbecue?"

"Tony!"

"Kristin," he said. "It's not in our budget to buy expensive backyard furniture."

Heading outside, I paced back and forth across the empty brick patio. *Think, Kristin. Think. You need a place for people to gather comfortably. It needs to be welcoming and practical. And it can't break the bank. Guests shouldn't sit formally, but casually, for conversation.*

I pressed my fingertips hard into my temples, trying to squeeze an answer out of my cluttered brain.

Casual. Like a picnic.

A picnic table. The thought came quickly and with resolution. Then doubt. Where on earth was I going to get a picnic table on such short notice? October was hardly prime picnic season, even in Austin, Texas.

I hurried inside to my laptop and did a quick search on Google for picnic tables.

"Well, how about that?" I caught myself talking aloud. At the top of my search screen was a seventy-two-inch southern yellow pine picnic table at Lowe's. I added two tables to my cart, opted for the convenient next-day delivery, and clicked Order Now. Crisis solved.

The next morning a delivery truck pulled to the side of my house. Two burly men came to the front door and asked where I wanted them to put the tables.

I followed the men outside and saw they had already unloaded one of the two picnic tables and left it in the front yard near the magnolia tree before realizing it might be a good idea to find out exactly where the heavy wooden tables were headed. I stopped abruptly, barely able to catch my breath when I saw the table sitting in my front yard.

"Oh!" I cupped my hands over my mouth, fingertips resting at the tip of my nose, as in prayer and shock.

"Ma'am, are you okay?" the delivery man asked.

"Oh, yes, sorry." I couldn't take my eyes off the picnic table.

"Where do you want the table?" He wiped his brow with a bandana.

"Right there," I whispered without thinking.

"Here? So close to the street?"

"Yes. *No!*" I slowly came back into the moment. "No. Sorry. I need them in the backyard." In that moment, I knew. As soon as the party was over, I was going to move that picnic table back to the front yard where it belonged.

I've been waiting for that table all my life.

But would the family agree?

At dinner the next night, I waited for the right moment to casually bring it up.

"After the party, what if we put one of the new picnic tables out front, under the magnolia tree, and used it as a gathering place?"

"A picnic table in the front yard?" Our eldest daughter, Anna, seemed intrigued, so I pressed in.

"Why not? What if this is the way we are supposed to live—as front yard people?"

Our son, Will, nodded. "Way to go, Mom. Doing your part to keep Austin weird."

He didn't sway me. I barreled on, painting scenarios. What if we moved our afternoon snacks, bubble blowing, messy art projects, barbecue suppers, and all our *backyard* activities to the *front yard*?

"Could we have lemonade stands?" Our youngest, Sarah, smiled eagerly.

"Yes, baby!"

"It's kinda dull looking now," Anna, an artist, observed.

"We could paint it," Ellie, our middle daughter, added quickly.

"Absolutely. Something bright and cheery." My heart was racing with their encouragement.

I crawled in bed late that night exhausted but hopeful. I snuggled close to Tony and asked him what he thought of the front-yard table idea.

Reassuringly, he kissed me good night. "I think you've already made up your mind."

I smiled and squeezed his hand. "I know it sounds crazy, but I've been waiting for that table all my life."

Spicy Pecans

My grandmother always set out a small bowl of nuts when company came over. One day I asked her about the dozen or so cans of mixed nuts in the pantry. She said, "Well, nuts were on sale, and I like to be ready when the gals stop by. It doesn't matter what you serve, just make sure you always put out a little something for your guests."

In honor of my grandmother's practical wisdom, I keep a can of nuts in the pantry, just in case. When I have time, I make our family's Spicy Pecan recipe. Trust me, these nuts are worth the minutes they take to make!

2 cups pecan halves

4 tablespoons (1/2 stick) butter

3 tablespoons soy sauce (or gluten-free tamari)

5 dashes Tabasco

1/2 teaspoon salt

Preheat oven to 300 degrees. Place pecans and butter on a rimmed baking sheet. Bake for 30 minutes, stirring occasionally to make sure all the pecans are coated in melted butter. In a small bowl stir together the soy sauce, Tabasco, and salt. Add warm pecans to soy sauce mixture and stir until coated. Drain pecans on paper towels. Store in refrigerator (in glass works best).

Simple Sautéed Apples

Encouraged by Ludmilla, I wondered if I could create a simple dish for my family without a recipe or going to the grocery store. Could I use ingredients I had on hand, just a few, and trust that something wonderful would result? It worked.

Hospitality doesn't have to be a big production. Try it! Open up your pantry and see what's right in front of you and turn it into an abundant offering of love.

4 tablespoons butter, 1/2 stick

2 apples, cored and sliced

1 tablespoon brown sugar

1/2 tablespoon cinnamon

Vanilla ice cream

In a skillet over low flame, sauté apples in butter, brown sugar, and cinnamon until apples are soft and slightly caramelized, about 10 minutes. Serve warm over vanilla ice cream.

4

KEEP IT SIMPLE

There is no greatness where there is
not simplicity, goodness, and truth.

Leo Tolstoy

ave you ever had that feeling deep in your core, *This is it?* From the moment I saw the picnic table, *I knew.* I believed with all my heart this ordinary, outdoor table could be the answer to the restless wondering and worry about how to offer hospitality in a meaningful and simple way.

Like a schoolgirl in love, I declared my intention to be a front yard person to the world. Maybe that's a *slight* exaggeration, but I did share the idea of putting a picnic table in my front yard with family and friends. And neighbors. And the random woman

in line at the grocery store. And on my blog, Twitter, Facebook, Instagram, and basically with anyone else who would listen.

It was a magical time. Full of hope, my imagination danced with all the possible ways we might gather at the front-yard picnic table. I invited friends and neighbors to weigh in on what color we should paint the table. Creative input came from near and far, but what struck me was how quickly the idea of a front-yard picnic table was resonating with people. It was as if people were transported in their minds to a simpler time when running barefoot through green grass, sipping homemade lemonade from the stand next door, and chatting in the driveway with old Mr. Smith were part of the daily rhythm of life.

I couldn't wait to get our table painted and set up out front. In the end I went with my favorite color—turquoise! My mother, Mia, who has an uncanny knack of picking colors, brought over paint samples narrowed down to two shades. Both looked fabulous to me, so I picked Nifty Turquoise because I loved the name as much as the color. We were ready to go.

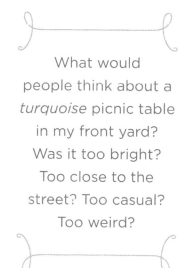

What would people think about a *turquoise* picnic table in my front yard? Was it too bright? Too close to the street? Too casual? Too weird?

Then doubt showed up like an unexpected guest. All the what-ifs clogged my mind. What would people think about a *turquoise* picnic table in my front yard? Was it too bright? Too close to the street? Too casual? Too weird? Worst of all, I grappled with the underlying fear of rejection: What if no one came?

I needed a little reassurance, so I called my friend Kimberley. We bounced ideas back and forth, affirming the ways the Turquoise Table would solve the biggest obstacles we faced when trying to bring people together. "It's like a baby step between doing nothing and having a big ol' party," she said.

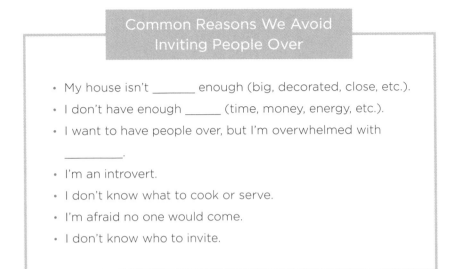

Common Reasons We Avoid Inviting People Over

- My house isn't _____ enough (big, decorated, close, etc.).
- I don't have enough _____ (time, money, energy, etc.).
- I want to have people over, but I'm overwhelmed with _____.
- I'm an introvert.
- I don't know what to cook or serve.
- I'm afraid no one would come.
- I don't know who to invite.

"It certainly eliminates the hassle, right? You can just focus on being present with friends."

"Absolutely. You don't have to worry about cleaning the house or making a fancy meal. And you avoid the panic when someone unexpectedly drops by. Just head outside and leave the laundry on the couch!"

I could feel my resolve return. "You're right. I'm counting on you to keep me accountable, friend." Now I really had to follow through, because Kimberley *would* follow up. No backing out now.

KEEP IT SIMPLE

OUR FIRST MORNING AT THE TURQUOISE TABLE

If only the rain would stop. It had been pouring for a solid week, and our freshly painted Turquoise Table was still in the garage.

Thursday morning the weather finally cleared. I knew it was the day. I convinced our yard guys to move the Turquoise Table from the garage to its spot under the magnolia tree in our front yard. It was now or never.

I had zero plans for what to do once I was at the table, so I began grabbing things—my computer, a journal, some pens, my phone, and the most essential: a mug of coffee. I went outside and sat at the new table, faced the street, and opened my laptop.

Try these journal prompts while enjoying your first day at the Turquoise Table.

- What's important to me about meeting my neighbors?
- What was your neighborhood like growing up?
- Dare to dream what your current neighborhood looks like a year from now. Describe what you see.

I was far enough from the house the WiFi didn't connect, so I really was unplugged at the table. I felt the tension of needing to fill the space around me to drown out the naysayers in my head ("this table's bright and too close to the street . . ."); it was all so foreign—the quiet alone time, sitting outside in the front yard, the agenda-less waiting. I began to doodle away the doubts in my journal.

MEETING A NEIGHBOR

It couldn't have been more than fifteen minutes before I noticed a woman out for a walk, headed my way. I'd never seen her before in the neighborhood. As she got a little closer, I could see she was holding something. It appeared to be a flyer—nothing more than a piece of junk mail.

When she got within earshot, she slowed down. I looked up and smiled, hiding that awkward split-second before someone spoke first.

"I noticed your bright table," she said. "I like it, and the red flowers are pretty. It reminds me of my fifth-grade elementary school photo. I wore a red turtleneck and a turquoise sweater."

The turquoise is working! We struck up a friendly conversation.

She stood with one foot in the street and one foot on the curb—almost within arm's reach. She said she was delivering a piece of junk mail that landed in her mailbox by mistake. Now, I don't know about you, but she's a better person than I am, because I would not have taken the time to deliver a piece of junk mail to a neighbor I didn't know.

Then she confided, "What I really needed was to get out of the house for a breath of fresh air." We went on to chat about normal, everyday things. We traded notes on lawn services, and she said her family was doing minor renovations and asked if I could recommend a handyman. For thirty minutes, our conversation flowed. Despite all my worries, fears, and hesitations, on the very first day at the table I had met a complete stranger who lives four doors down from me.

Do you know? In many cultures turquoise symbolizes friendship.

Susan went on to deliver the flyer to its proper address, then back home, and I sat in awe of the realization that an ordinary picnic table painted turquoise and a throwaway piece of junk mail had brought us together. Could it really be that simple?

SIMPLY SHOWING UP

As someone who struggles with wanting things perfect, I fall into the trap of making things harder than necessary. If this first experience at the table was any indication of the freedom from analysis paralysis—all that overthinking, overplanning, overdoing things when I end up doing nothing—I couldn't wait to do it again.

Maybe meeting Susan was a fluke, but it sure felt like affirmation to me. I couldn't wait to call Kimberley.

"I did it! I sat at the table and met a neighbor!"

"Of course you did," she said, much more confident than I was.

"I didn't do anything but show up. When Susan walked by it was surreal, almost like out of a movie."

"Be careful what you wish for," Kimberley said.

"What do you mean?" I wasn't processing the morning clearly yet.

"Looks like your obsession with Ludmilla is turning into reality. The Turquoise Table is your answered prayer."

That's the beauty of friends. Kimberley was already two steps ahead of me, seeing clearly what was still a blur to me. Ludmilla had painted the picture of how simple hospitality could be; taking it outside to a picnic table simplified it even more.

What if the answer was just to show up? I certainly didn't solve world peace or master the art of hospitality, but I did meet Susan. And that's a start.

Will another neighbor show up the next time I sit at the Turquoise Table? I had no way of knowing, but I was excited to head out there and await the possibilities. If I could meet one neighbor, why couldn't I meet them all?

So show up, we did. That very week the kids and I started doing normal activities like homework outside. I didn't make a big deal about it, but when the opportunity to sit outside at the Turquoise Table made sense, we took it. One afternoon a woman driving by stopped, rolled down her car window, and asked about

the flowers I had put in an old tin pitcher on the table. She asked if they were fake flowers. Indeed they were—fake as fake can be, straight from the craft store. Even though we live near the center of town, our neighborhood has a huge population of deer roaming free. Real flowers would have been chomped up by our woodland creatures in no time. I never officially met this woman, but she said she was off to buy some faux flowers to brighten up a table on her front porch.

Other days we waved at people walking by with their dogs, striking up friendly chatter with people who were beginning to look familiar. With simple interactions we were establishing presence. The kids decided to put candy out in a basket with a cute handmade sign that said, "Please enjoy!" We ate casual suppers at the Turquoise Table and enjoyed the nods and smiles of curious passersby. Best of all? Technology stayed inside in the iBasket. A bustling activity hub, the table was truly a place to unplug and connect.

The table had become such a regular part of our routine, I began to make mental note of practical items I could set aside to keep life easy when I wanted to head out to the table. I found an extra basket and began filling it with things I already had on hand. I put in a deck of cards and some coloring books for the kids. I keep the basket full of items on a shelf in the laundry room so everyone knows these are special items for the table.

In anticipation of someone dropping by, I added an unopened can of nuts from the pantry, cute napkins I had stuffed in a drawer waiting for the perfect occasion, and a box of my favorite tea. That way I was prepared to welcome guests without going overboard. How easy is that?

Unplug and Use an iBasket

Encourage your family and friends to unplug and connect at the table by placing their phones in a basket while you're eating dinner or enjoying time together at the Turquoise Table. Don't forget to toss yours in, too!

- Find a basket, cookie tin, or bowl. Get creative and use what you have—one friend uses an old fish bowl.
- Place your iBasket in a high traffic and convenient area of your home. Our iBasket is near the dinner table close to the front door.
- Add chargers so friends leave at 100 percent.
- Establish a reasonable screen-free time that works for your friends and family.
- Thank your family and friends for the gift of being present.

Set Aside These Everyday Items for Visits at Your Turquoise Table

After three years of having the table out, I have learned to keep it simple. I have a Turquoise Table basket where I keep a few supplies on hand to grab and go to the table. It's more about being organized and prepared than perfect. Now I don't have to race around trying to remember where I stashed the leftover cups from the last get-together. I simply grab what I need from the basket and head out.

- Plastic cups
- Water pitcher
- Cute napkins—from birthday parties or the ones you were tempted to re-gift!
- Tea, lemonade, or flavored water packets
- A journal to keep track of friends and neighbors who stop by
- A small stash of nuts, candy, or chocolate

ACTIVITY

Take the first step: move a table outside. Whatever your normal routine is, try it in the front yard! For just a few minutes (I started with thirty) read the mail, write a note to a friend, or journal outside at your table. Don't be discouraged if no one walks by; enjoy the gift of time unplugged at the table. You'll be surprised what you notice.

Creative Picnic Table Ideas

"I painted an old door turquoise, put it on saw horses, and found some folding chairs at a thrift shop. It's simple, and I loved the DIY project."

Meg, South Carolina

"We had an old iron table and four chairs in the backyard. I freshened it up with a can of turquoise paint and put it out front."

Amy, Texas

"I found a table and chairs on the side of the road, painted them turquoise, and put them in my front yard. So welcoming, and my neighbors love it!"

Lisa, Illinois

A Turquoise Table Story

When Brooke and her family moved to Austin, they didn't know anyone in their new neighborhood. They came from a tight-knit community, and she was eager to put down roots and get to know people. Not long after the move, Brooke heard about the Turquoise Table, and she just *knew*. She knew she wanted to have a Turquoise Table as a means to connect with her new neighbors. She knew spending time around the table would turn neighbors into friends. And she knew just how to make it happen.

Stacked in the corner of the garage in their newly built house was a pile of leftover building materials. An accidental delivery of wood that was never picked up by the builder sat unused and burdensome. After hearing about the Turquoise Table, Brooke asked her husband if he could build a table out of that wood, and he agreed to see how much of it could be used. It turned out they were only one board shy of a completed table! Almost exactly the amount of wood needed for the table was right there all along.

"That wood had been delivered to our house three months

before we even knew what we were going to do with it," Brooke said. "It seems like God knew full well that we would use it to build our table and reach out to our neighbors."

Brooke's two young sons helped her prime and paint the table turquoise, except for that one additional board that had to be purchased. She placed that board in the center of the table and painted it burnt orange to signify the family's move to Austin—the home of the University of Texas Longhorns. Once the table was placed in the front yard, the family made a point of getting out there frequently, though not on any set schedule or plan. Over the months they have met many of their neighbors and started gathering to share snacks, meals, and conversation. Just recently Brooke texted many of her new friends to let them know that she was setting up a Slip 'N Slide in the front yard for the kids and welcomed everyone to join in the fun. Several families came and cooled off in the spray, laughing as the kids slid across the yard.

"The Turquoise Table has been the center of many wonderful events already," said Brooke. "It's given us the opportunity to make new friends for our children and ourselves in our new neighborhood, and enabled other families to do the same."

Brooke's Turquoise Table also inspired one of her friends back in Las Vegas to have a table of her own. Neighborhood lots are significantly smaller in that area, so fitting a picnic table in the front yard wasn't feasible. Instead, Brooke's friend now has a Turquoise "Bistro" Table out front that better fits the scale of her yard while still enabling new neighborhood friendships to flourish. A smaller table can still produce big connections.

Front Yard People are emerging, both next door and a thousand miles away. That forgotten wood in the garage has definitely been transformed into something magical.

Homemade Vanilla Latte

Every morning I make the same vanilla latte. A little bit of milk, flavored with Mexican vanilla and Stevia. I whip it with an inexpensive milk frother and voilà—a homemade vanilla latte. It's the drink I carried with me to the table that very first day. By taking a moment to enrich my ritual cup of morning coffee, I gave myself permission to savor time at the Turquoise Table.

1 cup coffee brewed (or shot of espresso)

¼ cup milk

1–2 drops of Mexican vanilla extract

Stevia, or sweetener to taste

Brew coffee. Warm milk in microwave or on stove. Add 1 to 2 drops of Mexican vanilla and Stevia. Froth with a hand frother. Pour coffee in mug, and top with warm vanilla milk.

5

COME TO THE TABLE

Our culture is hungry for table time.

Leonard Sweet

Whether you're the spontaneous type or you like a little planning, the table can fit your personality. It doesn't have to be complicated—you can invite anyone to the table, whether old friends or new. Who are the first people who pop into your mind? Invite them.

One of the first official gatherings at our table was serendip-itous, which suits my personality. Our neighbor Amy was at a children's birthday party sitting with a group of moms when the woman next to her said, "Have y'all heard about the lady who put a turquoise table in her front yard?"

Amy responded, "Um, *yes*! She's my neighbor, Kristin Schell."

The woman asked if she could meet me. Amy immediately began texting me their conversation and asked if we could get together.

I responded, "Invite her to coffee at the table."

"When?"

"Thursday at 9:30 a.m.?"

A few minutes later, the answer came through: "We're on and she's bringing a friend."

Thursday morning came. I made a pot of coffee, glanced at the clock, and realized I had just enough time to take a shower before heading out to the Turquoise Table. I almost tripped over a mess of shoes the kids left by the door, but shrugged it off. I didn't have to clean the house—my guests would be outside.

I walked out to the table with a tray of mugs and a carafe of coffee and waited for everyone to arrive. Julie, her friend Kimberly, and Amy showed up a few minutes later, making four of us at the table that morning. I only knew Amy and loved that I was meeting the other women for the first time.

We sat down, and Julie wasted no time. She whacked the table palms down like she was claiming it. "Girl! I love this idea so much I ordered my picnic table after the birthday party, and it was delivered and painted the next day."

She knew so little about the Turquoise Table, but her enthusiasm was evident—and contagious. Kimberly laughed. "Me too! I did the same thing. I still need to paint mine, though."

Julie asked, "What's the back story? How did you think of this?"

I poured everyone more coffee, settled in, and told them about Ludmilla's ministry of presence, and how relationships can be nurtured when we take time to sit down and connect with one another at the table. "Ludmilla modeled how powerful the simple act of being available to others can be."

"I've got chills," Julie said.

The conversation flowed into sharing our own frustrations and longings. We expressed our desire to get to know each other and the neighbors around us and live with more intention, but conceded how hard it was with all the busy day-to-day activities. We threw it all out on the table: asking questions about how to manage jobs, family, health concerns. With little or no margins in our lives, the idea of being present seemed out of reach.

And yet, as I looked around the table, we were doing it. We were already being a little bit like Ludmilla to one another. We hadn't prepared; we hadn't planned. We just showed up. It was the first step of opening our lives to one another.

The whole morning went like that—one series of head nods after another, sharing the highs and lows of where we were in the midst of raising kids, trying to be good wives, dealing with the struggle of getting dinner on the table when we spend more time in our cars than our kitchens. We opened up about the worries of raising our children in the digital age and getting it "right" as parents. We reflected on our own childhoods and the hard place of watching our parents age.

Without thinking about it, we skipped past the shallow and dove right into the deep end. We had gone from strangers to friends in zero to sixty seconds flat. Maybe the art of conversation isn't lost after all. We just need more practice at it.

I'm a busy working mother, and truthfully my house is a cozy retreat that is mostly reserved for downtime with my family. It's also a fairly small house, so having large events in my home would be out of the question. But with my Turquoise Table, I can host friends and neighbors regularly without the pressure of having them inside.

Nicole, Texas

CONVERSATION LEADS TO CONNECTION

What we were experiencing wasn't idle chit-chat on the sideline of a soccer field. It wasn't hurried pleasantries waved in a grocery store line. There was something special about what was happening. Sitting outside face-to-face at the Turquoise Table offered opportunity for organic conversation without boundaries.

Could it be that like the old village well, this ordinary table—in a world of all the technology and busyness and modern conveniences—creates a gathering place where real conversation can take place? In the midst of it all, the table becomes a sanctuary, a break from iDevices and a return to eye contact.

I can imagine women sharing similar struggles and stories around the village well hundreds of years ago. It's what women do.

We're drawn to each other and our stories and through that, experience oneness. It's how community is built: layer by layer, struggle by struggle, story by story.

It's why we come to the table, and these women and I were doing it.

And I didn't even have to clean the house.

CHOOSING HOSPITALITY

We've got to debunk the myth that hospitality is the same as entertainment. Genuine hospitality begins with opening our lives. It's just as important to open up our lives as it is our homes, and sharing who we are is far more important than sharing what we bake. In fact, sharing our hearts is more important than sharing a plate of chocolate chip cookies, though cookies might soften us up to share the pieces of us that are shy. Hospitality begins in the heart, not the oven.

It all starts with inviting people to come to the table. Hospitality is always about the people, not the presentation. That's what the neighbors one street over, on Glen Ridge Drive, found out.

At the same time I was wrestling with God, wondering how to create community, two blocks over, neighbors I didn't know yet had similar longings. Shannon, Mary Beth, Mandy, and Amy are all mothers of young children longing for deeper connection, and let's be honest, adult conversation and beverages. Shannon heard about the idea of Front Yard Friday and suggested they give it a try. The concept of Front Yard Friday is simple: invite neighbors to join

you for a casual get-together on a Friday evening in your front yard. *Easy enough*, they thought, and that week the four families hosted the first Front Yard Friday. All they did was show up in Mary Beth's front yard with a cooler and pizza. The next go-round they created a sign for the front yard to let other neighbors know about the gathering. When the news of the Friday-evening gatherings made it to our street, we combined efforts and started

having Front Yard Fridays at the Turquoise Table. Now there are three streets in our neighborhood that are all connected.

After a delightful first morning at the table with Julie, Amy,

Ways to Kick-start Your Table Gatherings

- PJs in the 'Hood: Invite moms to bring their kids over so they can run around and blow off energy before bedtime.
- Donuts and Coffee: Some weekday morning while waiting for the bus or on a Saturday morning, sit outside and offer donuts and coffee to whoever passes by.
- Girl Scout Cookie Sales: No brainer. You've got 'em, sell 'em.
- Lemonade Stand
- Soup on Sundays
- Cocoa and Cookies to kick off the Christmas holidays
- Bible Study
- Happy Hour
- Clean-Out-the-Fridge Party
- Movie Night
- S'mores Party
- Star Gazing: One family invites neighbors to view the constellations through their telescope.

and Kimberly, one of us glanced at the time. We had been talking for over an hour. We wrapped it up by brainstorming ideas we could all take back home. Collectively we came up with new ideas and existing activities that could incorporate the Turquoise Table.

Soon we all had enough ideas for everyone to take back to their own tables. Before saying good-bye, we passed around our iPhones and added each other's contact information and agreed to stay in touch so we could share stories of what was happening at our different tables.

As I watched each of them get up and head back home, I thought about how grateful I was for these women. We'd formed a buddy system, linking arms as we ventured into something new together.

What started as one table expanded to four. Four new friends. Just like that!

We just had our first gathering for our Turquoise Table! I was worried there would be awkward moments of silence and that I would have to entertain; turns out I just had to provide a space. We came together not knowing one another and left as old friends. We had a blast!

Melissa, North Carolina

ACTIVITY

Invite a couple of friends or neighbors over to share with them the idea of the Turquoise Table. Together plan your first Turquoise Table gathering.

A Turquoise Table Story

Growing up in a small town in the 1980s, Steph remembers the sense of community surrounding her neighborhood. Neighbors looked out for each other because they knew one another, not just by face, but by name. Families grilled dinner together, children played in the front yards, and neighbors helped one another.

"Where I'm from we didn't have fences unless it was a chain-link dog run," said Steph. "We had a general idea when people were home because we could see them coming and going. In fact, as a kid, the only reason to really be inside our house was to eat, sleep, or do homework."

When Steph and her husband moved into their first home nearly ten years ago, they had visions of neighbors barbecuing on summer evenings and sharing coffee on chilly mornings out on the front lawns. They quickly realized alleyways, no front porches, and high fence lines prevented them from seeing their neighbors, let alone knowing them.

Steph knew she could continue to dream about the kind of

neighborhood they wanted, or she could roll up her sleeves and get busy meeting her neighbors. When she heard about the Turquoise Table, it was just the jump-start she needed.

Knowing it would be easier if she had a friend on board, Steph shared the idea with her neighbor Laura. They both got Turquoise Tables and began to coordinate their first gatherings. Steph posted invites on Facebook, and Laura and her kids walked door-to-door with flyers. Because this sort of friendly gesture is no longer commonplace, many neighbors were surprised by the invitation. One even questioned Laura's motivation, assuming that she must be selling something or raising money for a cause. She had to explain politely that the only agenda was creating new friendships.

"It's clear that people are craving real community but just don't know how to make it happen," said Laura. "Busy lives don't enable us to spend time with our neighbors anymore unless we are intentional about it."

While Steph and Laura collaborate and support each other, the community around their respective tables looks very different.

"I live on a busy street," Steph said. "There's lots of activity and opportunity for spontaneous interaction with people passing by or coming home from work at the bus stop." Steph plans festive but casual events in her front yard. In the hot summer months she puts out the Slip 'N Slide and has plenty of snacks and popsicles for the neighborhood kids. At Christmas she organizes a neighborhood caroling party. One year there were so many neighbors who showed up that instead of caroling door-to-door (no one was home; all the neighbors had joined in!), they decided to stay at the Turquoise Table and sing carols for all the people passing by.

"These kind of neighborhood activities are refreshing for people," said Steph. "It takes them back to childhood. We don't go overboard. I'm not here to impress; we're just providing an opportunity for normal, easy fun."

Laura and her family live a couple blocks away from Steph, but their house is tucked away on a quiet street. Laura takes a more one-on-one approach. She and her family like to have neighbors over for casual front-yard suppers. Pizza, potluck, it really doesn't matter what's for dinner, the neighbors just enjoy each other's company. Recently, leftovers made for a reason to gather at the Turquoise Table.

"We had two pans of lasagna left over from a luncheon one Sunday," Laura said. "I wasn't interested in eating lasagna every day that week, so I invited the neighbors over for supper."

The two friends have found it meaningful to support each other in their mutual quest to love their neighbors.

"Even if you have a friend who isn't ready or can't put a table in their lawn, I really do think it's important to have someone to team with," Steph said. "It's encouraging to know Laura is there for me. She'll bring her neighbors to my front-yard gatherings and we show up at hers. Laura always has food!" Steph said.

Both women agree: "Serve food at the Turquoise Table, and you will meet your neighbors!"

Turquoise Table M&M Cookies

Always feel free simply to carry out a pitcher of water and some plastic cups. But if you have the time, try this crowd-pleasing cookie recipe shared by Colleen Enos especially for our Front Yard People community. Colleen said this recipe was given to her years ago by her mother-in-law, who is remembered for her genuine hospitality. "She would be thrilled to know her cookie recipe continues to be used to bring joy and a little sweetness to people," Colleen said. One woman makes these cookies every Monday morning to have on hand for visitors who might drop by her Turquoise Table. Try them for your first gathering!

- 1 cup shortening
- 1/2 cup white sugar
- 1 cup brown sugar
- 2 teaspoons vanilla extract
- 2 large eggs
- 1 teaspoon baking soda
- 2 1/4 cups all-purpose flour

1 teaspoon salt

1 ¹/₂ cups turquoise M&M's, divided

Heat oven to 350 degrees. In a stand mixer cream shortening, white sugar, brown sugar, eggs, and vanilla thoroughly. In a large bowl sift together flour, baking soda, and salt. Add the flour mixture gradually to shortening mixture and mix well. Stir in 1 cup of M&M's. Reserve remaining candy for decorating. Drop tablespoons on a parchment-lined cookie sheet. Place 4 to 5 turquoise M&M's on top of each cookie. Bake for 10 minutes, or until golden around the edges.

I like these cookies slightly underbaked. Turquoise Table M&M Cookies freeze well too.

6

Gather Small,
Love Deep

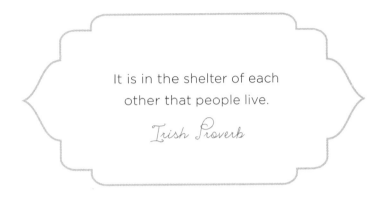

It is in the shelter of each
other that people live.

Irish Proverb

Our neighbor Elizabeth, who's in her eighties, walks her dog, Clyde, on our street three times a day. I knew Elizabeth and her husband, the Colonel, from our annual Parties in the Cove, but I didn't know much about them, other than that our garage doors face each other. We'd wave and strike up casual conversations on Thursday mornings as we were pulling out trash bins in the cul-de-sac, but that was about it.

After spending time at the Turquoise Table, I started noticing a rhythm and cadence to the neighborhood. There's a woman who runs by our house every day at noon. She doesn't live on our street; we're just on her running path. She wears earphones and has an iPod wrapped around her left arm. One week she was gone, probably on vacation. When she jogged by the following week, I felt relieved knowing she was back in her routine. Another woman walks by the table every day with two gorgeous white Samoyeds. One morning I noticed someone else walking them. *What's going on?* The next day, when the unfamiliar woman passed by again, I asked. Turned out the owner of the dogs fell and broke her leg in two places. Her friend offered to walk the dogs and keep them on a routine. I sent my well wishes and prayers for a speedy recovery back with her friend. I was surprised by the compassion I felt for this stranger. Hearing her story created an unexpected bond in my heart. It wasn't just me who was establishing a presence, sitting at the table; these people were now present in my life too.

> We learn the skills of hospitality in small increments of daily faithfulness.
>
> *Christine Pohl, Making Room*

I knew what was in the works two weeks before the house down the street went on the market. It wasn't hard to figure out when a painter, a plumber, and a gutter man showed up all in the same week. Anyone who can pull off that coup has an agenda beyond a weekend "Honey-Do" punch list. Sure enough, when I asked my neighbor, she confirmed a For Sale sign would be in the yard the next day. You can tell what people are doing if you take time to notice.

But does noticing matter? It seems so passive, and I struggle with the concept of *being* versus *doing.* My default mode is "to do"—host fun parties, buy dog treats for all the neighborhood pups, strike up a conversation with every passerby. Our society equates busyness with success, and I internalize that to mean the more I do, the bigger the difference I will make. Slowing down to a halt long enough and often enough to notice that a stranger who jogs by is suddenly missing feels at first like maybe a colossal waste of time. However, it was in those seemingly insignificant moments of sitting at the table, observing and noticing—sometimes in deafening silence—I was learning about my neighborhood.

ORDINARY MOMENTS MATTER

I started using the phrase "gather small and love deep" long before I fully realized what it meant. Intuitively I knew the Turquoise Table was perfectly designed for four to six people—small gatherings. And being at a table, facing each other and sitting side by side, would allow an intimacy to listen and have real conversations. What I didn't anticipate was the importance of these small and ordinary moments.

At first I would ask myself, doubting, "Is it enough?" Is it enough to know my neighbors by name? To spend an hour simply having coffee with only a handful of people? Does it matter if all I do is nod my head with pursed lips and a wrinkled brow while a friend shares her heart? Is it enough to wave at the jogger? Does inviting half a dozen people for donuts in the front yard matter? With the magnitude of problems in the world, do these small gatherings at the table matter?

It took a while for my heart to catch up to my head. My impulsive side—you know, the one that painted the picnic table turquoise and plopped it in the front yard—believed without a shred of doubt that being present in the front yard matters. I recognize it now as faith—not something I control or do on my own, but God's gift to me—to keep going, to keep sitting at the table, to keep loving my neighbors as He intends for us all to do. I was hearing faint whispers of encouragement as I realized God was saying, "It matters to Me. When you show up, I'm at work."

Hospitality always feels small when you hold it in your hands. It's not until you let it go, released like an offering, that you see how extravagant and hallowed it is. Sometimes I don't "feel" anything happening, which, in our instant gratification and quick-fix society, feels like failure. Building community, investing in the lives right in front of us, requires us to take the long view. Eugene Peterson refers to this type of relationship building as "a long obedience in the same direction."

One day, inspired by Elizabeth and the other dog walkers, I filled two dog bowls with water and set them next to the Turquoise Table. I pointed out the water bowls to Elizabeth the next time she and Clyde walked by. She sat down at the table with me while Clyde lapped up the water. She said Clyde had been sick and was recovering from surgery. The veterinarian gave him a good prognosis, but he got tired more quickly on their walks. Elizabeth shared how grateful she was for a place to sit in the shade and rest with Clyde.

Try this: Ask people how they are doing. Then create the space to listen actively while they answer.

After three years of talking to Elizabeth on her walks with Clyde, I realize how much we've come to know about each other. We share stories and prayers for health and family members. And we keep a good eye out for one another. If I don't see her out walking Clyde, I know to go ring the doorbell and just

Front Yard People Pups

Dogs are a great way to meet new neighbors. It's so much easier to say, "What a cute dog!" than "Hi, my name is Kristin!" If it hadn't been for Clyde, I might not have the friendship I do with Elizabeth. Try these tips to invite dogs to your table, too!

- Put a water bowl outside near your Turquoise Table.
- Set a small jar of dog treats on the table.
- Make a small sign to let walkers know water and treats are available for their dogs.
- Attach a leash hook to the table so owners can sit and visit while keeping their dogs safe.

say, "I'm checking on you." When we are out of town, I ask another neighbor to put out water for Clyde and the other dogs. It's simple. And it started with the small act of noticing and being present.

God is teaching me the ministry of presence. Just like I first saw Ludmilla model. I didn't make any drastic changes to my schedule—I'm still the Queen of Crazy. But I've come to savor these moments of being outside and available at the Turquoise Table. By being at the table, I'm saying to anyone who passes by, and to God too, "I'm available." It's a promise. It's an extension of the "yes" I said when I put out the table.

The Turquoise Table

THURSDAYS AT THE TABLE

I wasn't the only one doing the noticing. Neighbors noticed I was outside too. I decided to dedicate Thursday mornings to making my time at the table more intentional. I'm out there most Thursdays, hanging out during what neighbors call my "table hours." Some mornings are planned and I invite friends to join me in advance. Other mornings I leave open to see who might show up. If no one stops by, I enjoy the gift of time to do things like write, read a book, or work on a Bible study. Some mornings I sit still and pray, knowing it might be the only quiet time during my day. I trust the time will be filled however it needs to be that morning.

LEARNING TO LISTEN

They say the way to a man's heart is through his stomach. Well, the way to a friend's heart is through your ears. The most important lesson in being present is listening. And this much I know is true—whether people are invited or spontaneously show up to the Turquoise Table, they arrive ready to sit and talk. Real conversation is an invitation. It's the most authentic way we can say, "You matter."

I have to be honest, listening isn't a skill that comes easy for me. I'm a notorious interrupter. Sometimes instead of focusing on what the other person is saying, I'm planning what I'm going to say next. How awful is that? My poor listening skills affect my ability to remember. I'm always worried my memory's going because I can't remember a darned thing. The cure, for me, is learning to listen.

The Turquoise Table is a visible reminder of God's love. An invitation to welcome others into the mundane, everyday moments of our lives. The beauty of the table lies in its simplicity, making an easy way to be present and available to listen. People want to be heard. You will connect if you open your ears and your

Quiet Time at the Turquoise Table

I learned that mornings alone at the table are special gifts. In order to be present for our family, friends, and neighbors we must not ignore the importance of making room for quiet time with God. Take time to rest and be still at the table:

- Pray for your family.
- As you step out to nurture relationships in your community, ask for patience, protection, and provision.
- Pray for balance and boundaries with your time.
- Pray for your neighbors.

heart. Being present and listening is the foundation to hospitality. I had it backward for so long. I thought I had to master the art of fancy French cooking to make people feel welcome. I thought hospitality was about entertaining and preparing a fine feast. Don't get me wrong, delicious food will always be my love language, but learning to listen and be present is paramount if we are to take every opportunity to open our lives and homes to others.

> Listening is a form of spiritual hospitality by which you invite strangers to become friends, to get to know their inner selves more fully, and even to dare to be silent with you.
>
> *Henri Nouwen*

Start a Front Yard People journal. Jot down the comings and goings of your neighbors. I don't know about you, but if I don't write things down, I'll forget. I wish I had started a journal for the Turquoise Table sooner. Start noting some of these things in your journal:

- Names of neighbors and people you meet
- Names of spouses, children, grandchildren, pets
- Quick details about jobs, schools, hometowns
- Important dates coming up for friends and neighbors—birthdays, anniversaries, graduations
- Prayer requests
- Details about health status and surgeries
- Out-of-town dates

Tips for Listening

Practice being an active listener with these small but important steps. These pointers seem so obvious, I'm embarrassed to say how often I need reminding.

- Maintain eye contact.
- No interrupting.
- Wait your turn before speaking.
- Don't try to solve or fix the problem.
- Stay attentive.
- Be aware of your body language.
- Pay attention to what *isn't* being said.
- Smile with your eyes.
- Don't be afraid of silence.

My neighbor Nicole loves to use the phrase "tell me more." It gives permission for people to go beyond polite conversation and share deeper.

GATHER SMALL, LOVE DEEP

A Turquoise Table Story

Not long after she put a Turquoise Table in her own front yard, Julie began to wonder about ways she could make a difference in her community by being present at her table. She started paying attention to the people in her neighborhood—mostly young families with children. Julie is passionate about teaching her children the importance of giving back to different nonprofits in her community. She invited neighbors to brainstorm with her at the table and began by asking, "What needs can we meet in our neighborhood?"

Julie decided to host parties with a deeper purpose. She started by bringing neighbors together to learn about various nonprofits in their community and do an activity or take up a collection that would benefit that nonprofit. After one or two of these project-based parties, the gatherings at her Turquoise Table evolved into Parties with a Purpose. Now, each month, she and neighbors tackle something new. They've made shoes from old jeans for children in Uganda and blankets for mothers to swaddle their premature babies.

Recently, the group of compassionate moms decided to look a little closer to home and asked, "How can we love our neighbors, right here, right now?" With school about to start and an influx of more than three hundred refugee families to the neighborhood, the moms decided to extend a special welcome to the children from Sudan, Somalia, Afghanistan, Iraq, and Iran. They hosted a backpack and school supply drive. Word spread fast, and soon her Turquoise Table was covered with bright backpacks and new school supplies for the kids.

"Providing a new backpack and various school supplies not only helps prepare kids for school, but for the children of refugee families, it gives them some brand-new possessions to call

their very own," Julie said. "We want these children and their families to feel not just welcome but warmly embraced into our community and schools."

Debbie, who lives in Louisiana, also began wondering how she might use her Turquoise Table to connect with neighbors and get to know people in her new community.

> Artist gatherings and a full box of prayers. Loving your neighbors doesn't get much better than that.

"Our table started out like so many do," said Debbie. "My kids would hang out, my husband would work at the table, and neighbors would stop by. And that in itself was wonderful. But then I got to thinking that I could really take this to the next level."

A lifelong lover of the arts, Debbie quickly got involved in Shreveport's thriving art and music scene. Their home is located close to an art museum, one of the city's premier destinations. With her Turquoise Table so near the cultural center, Debbie felt she could not only continue to promote the arts but also provide a connection point for various types of art lovers (from hipsters to young families to empty-nesters) and for folks from various parts of town.

"Art and music draw people together, even those with

different views and backgrounds," she said. "So I started inviting several groups of people to use the Turquoise Table as part of their artistic events. I've hosted band parties and art shows, and it has been fantastic."

Then Debbie noticed another need. She wondered how she might be able to pray for her neighbors without an awkward, "Hi, my name is Debbie, may I pray for you?" conversation. She remembered an unused wooden box her kids built for a game they never got around to playing. She painted the wooden box, added some notecards and pens, made a Prayer Box sign, and put it outside on the Turquoise Table.

Debbie didn't expect much, but the next day she noticed the garbage man sitting at the table writing out a prayer request. A few days later, a truck driver stopped and took a photo of the Turquoise Table. Debbie doesn't know if he left a prayer request, but that didn't stop her from saying a prayer for him anyway.

"The prayer box has truly opened my eyes to the needs in my community. And changed my heart. Most of the cards don't have names, but God knows the details," Debbie said.

Debbie's prayer box stays full. Every few days she brings the prayer-filled pieces of paper inside and puts them on her refrigerator so her family can say prayers for their neighbors too. She's even enlisted the help of her Bible study group to help her keep up with the requests.

"Artist gatherings and a full box of prayers. Loving your neighbors doesn't get much better than that," said Debbie.

When we are present and begin to know our neighbors and the needs of the community by listening and being present, we see opportunities and ways transformation can begin to unfold in our communities.

Provençal Bistro Chicken

As I spend time in the front yard with neighbors and friends, I rely on my trusty slow cooker for time-saving family suppers. This riff on the French classic is simple and one of our family favorites.

8–10 boneless, skinless chicken thighs

Salt and black pepper to taste

2–3 tablespoons olive oil

2 tablespoons butter

2 onions, chopped

3–4 garlic cloves, minced

3 teaspoons dried thyme

1 cup red wine

1 (28-ounce) can diced tomatoes

Season the chicken with salt and pepper. In a large skillet heat the olive oil over medium heat. Add the chicken, in batches if necessary, and cook 5–6 minutes per side until browned.

Transfer the chicken to a slow cooker. Melt the butter in the cast-iron skillet, over medium-high heat. Add the onions, garlic, and thyme. Sauté until the onions are soft and translucent, about 5 minutes.

Add the wine and tomatoes. Scrape up all the brown bits from the bottom of the pan. Simmer until well combined, just 1 to 2 minutes. Pour the mixture over the chicken in the slow cooker.

Cover and cook on low for 6 to 8 hours.

7

Belonging at the Table

> There are no strangers here; only friends you have not met yet.
>
> *William Butter Yeats*

As the mother of teenagers, I hear my fair share of typical social woes—who's in, who's out, the hurt of not being invited to "the party," or the rejection when "there's no room for you" at the school lunch table. I die a hundred deaths holding the hand of my child listening to the all-too-familiar stories.

We've all felt it: the sting of not being included, the yearning to belong. Whether the pain of the circumstance is short-lived or long suffered, the loneliness of exclusion is hard to shake. Community is a basic need of humanity and the table—all tables—should be a place of inclusion.

Lately I've been sitting at the Turquoise Table overwhelmed with gratitude that people who were once strangers I now call by name. People who stop by and those who hang out regularly at the table are more than neighbors—they are friends. We've celebrated births, cheered at graduations, mourned the tragedy of illness and death, and in between it all we've shared the gift of ordinary days. I feel settled now. I know we belong in this neighborhood. With these people and at this table.

Community is a basic need of humanity and the table—all tables—should be a place of inclusion.

But it wasn't always that way.

For a very long time, I struggled to find my place. It began the fall of my seventh-grade year, in the second-floor hallway of middle school in Dallas, when I got beat up. A bully, whose name I never knew, asked me for lunch money. When I told her I didn't have any, she clocked me square in the jaw. I hurtled backward against the lockers and don't remember much after that. While I didn't sustain severe injuries, my mother's mama bear instincts prevailed and she withdrew me from school that very day.

A few weeks later, I showed up wearing a plaid skirt and saddle oxfords at the neighborhood Christian school. Part of our daily schedule was to attend the church service, but because I was from a different denomination, I was not allowed to participate in Communion. Day in and day out, for the remainder of my seventh- and eighth-grade years, I sat alone, unable to partake in Eucharist at the table. Sitting in that pew, feet dangling, watching all my friends take Communion was hard. I was excluded because of my religion. And, of all places, at church.

I felt like an outsider, excluded from the table. And not just any table—the Lord's Table.

I was confused, and worse—I was hurt. Unable to rationalize, I gave up on a God who I believed had surely given up on me. I locked up my faith and left it in that church in Dallas.

The next chapter in my life I traveled far and wide during what I call my Wanderlust Era. Driven by an insatiable curiosity, I spent more than a decade traveling on and off with study-abroad and foreign-exchange programs. I lived in the tiny village of Ornans, France, and spent a semester of college in Strasbourg, Austria. I traveled to East Berlin on an internship program before the Wall fell, and I journeyed with a collegiate exchange council to Irkutsk, Siberia—yes, Siberia.

A STRANGER AT FOREIGN TABLES

While I was busy trying to "find myself," God was busy orchestrating experiences that would shape and prepare me for the Turquoise Table. Ever the good Gardener, He was planting the seeds of hospitality in my heart. Looking back, I can connect the dots, like a road map, seeing where these seeds were planted. Almost all of them in a foreign land, at a common table.

Some of the most wonderful moments where I truly felt I belonged occurred when I was a complete stranger to my hosts. In the spring of 1990, I traveled to the former Soviet Union with a college program aimed at promoting goodwill among a younger generation during the thawing Cold War. News flash—it's cold in Siberia! The subzero temperatures, however, were easily forgotten inside the warmth of my friend Olga's home.

> When we open ourselves to the stranger, we open ourselves to the holy.

Our group of American and Russian students settled in one night for a festive and unforgettable dinner. Peering in from a frosty windowpane, you never would have known tensions were high between our nations. Or that despite the language and cultural barriers, we had little trouble communicating. Well into the wee hours of the morning, and long after the bowls of fish head soup had been cleared, we told stories, sang songs, and laughed like lifelong friends. I didn't speak a lick of Russian beyond a few key phrases, yet somehow our group managed to understand each other by leaning on those with a better command of the language and waiting, or not, for official translations.

Early on in the evening, Olga pulled me aside for a tour of her apartment. Pointing at a series of paintings on the wall, she explained her grandfather was exiled to Siberia. Perhaps a political dissident—I never fully understood—he was also a painter. She

told me the story of her family's life through the canvases her grandfather left behind. As the evening drew to a close, my friend gave me a gift—a watercolor of an iconic domed Russian church painted by her beloved *Dedushka*. In Russia, it is customary for the host and guest to exchange small gifts, but this was truly extravagant. Olga invited me in, not only to her table for an authentic meal, but into her life. We hugged through tears, knowing that no matter what the world told us, friendship between strangers is possible.

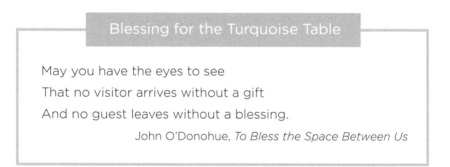

Blessing for the Turquoise Table

May you have the eyes to see
That no visitor arrives without a gift
And no guest leaves without a blessing.

John O'Donohue, *To Bless the Space Between Us*

LOVE OF STRANGERS

Years later I learned the word *hospitality* comes from two Greek roots: *philos*, which means "love," and *xenos*, which means "stranger." Hospitality is the love of strangers. When we take Romans 12:13 literally, we are to take every opportunity to open our lives and homes to others. We are to love others—friend, foe, neighbor, and stranger. Love and hospitality always go together.

Before we can be a good host, we must experience being a welcomed guest, and before we can create a place of belonging for others, we must believe we belong. For that, we must first know to whom we belong. We are able to love because we were first loved.

There are no insiders when everyone is outside at the Turquoise Table. All are welcome.

Because of my love of travel, I always thought I would go far and wide on missions. Never in a million years did I imagine God would ask me to serve in the most ordinary place of all: my front yard. That's right. God didn't send me to Africa. He didn't send me back to Russia. He sent me outside my front door right into my front yard. God gave me a table.

The table was a gift of redemption and reconciliation, given that the place I was excluded from long ago was the Communion table. He gave me a new one. Out of love and out of grace, God gave me a table. We know when He gives a gift, it's meant to be shared.

Once I was excluded, and now I belong.

That's what I want to give others.

We live in a world where people profile and label each other,

Strangers and Safety: History of Hospitality

The ancient practice of hospitality was born out of a need for safety. Traditional hospitality consisted of welcoming travelers, or strangers, into one's home by offering provision and protection. In the first century, safety became a paramount concern for Christian travelers. Because they were frequently persecuted and local inns were often dangerous, Christians relied on the hospitality of strangers for a place to sleep, meals, and safety.

size each other up. What if we shifted our focus to similarities? To welcoming one another, listening to stories, learning from one another? It's time to change the conversation. I believe most social ills can be healed or prevented by the simple act of talking to one another, face-to-face, at a common table.

We all need to be cautious of people with bad intentions. Use common sense and street smarts, wherever you live. But when you sit at the Turquoise Table, make sure all people feel welcome, no matter how young or old, no matter their mother tongue or attire, regardless of race or religion. Invite them to sit awhile. Serve something cold to drink. Share something simple—I once grabbed the fruit bowl off my counter and took it outside! Above all, listen.

ACTIVITY

When have you struggled to belong or felt excluded? Take some time to journal your memories and feelings. Did reading the stories of the people in the last chapter make you think of anyone in your community? Has God put anyone on your heart who might feel left out, who might not have intuitively been invited to the table—or might not feel comfortable walking up to say hello and ask to sit? Consider making room for that person and inviting her to the Turquoise Table.

Let guests at the table know they are welcome. You may be surprised at the delightful conversations you have, the new customs you learn, and the stories they have to share. Make a place where all feel comfortable and safe. Be situationally aware, of course, but try creating a place of peace as an alternative to the fear of the unknown that separates you from others.

Susan woke up one morning with leftover cookies from a big batch she'd made to welcome her son home from college for Christmas. After a few days with an abundance of cookies testing her willpower, she had to stop eating them, but hated to toss them in the garbage. In a spontaneous move, she texted several friends: "Come to the table in the morning for coffee and Christmas cookies."

This may not seem out of the ordinary until you consider a spur-of-the-moment gathering is out of character for Susan, a self-proclaimed introvert.

"I didn't let myself think about the fact that it was the worst possible time of the year to plan such a gathering," she said. Common sense told her no one would be able to fit in an impromptu gathering two weeks before Christmas, but the cookies had to go!

She also didn't overthink texting me. She saw my name in her contact list and thought, *Why not? The worst she can do is say no.*

The Turquoise Table

When I received Susan's text, my first instinct was, *Are you kidding? Christmas is almost here; it's the last week of school. I have a million things to do.*

My mind was whirling with excuses and how I didn't have time for coffee, but my fingers typed the message, "Thanks, I'd love to join you."

I didn't know Susan that well; in fact, I'd only met her once. And I had no idea who else would be at the table.

Later that day, I thought, *This is crazy, but why not show up to a stranger's house for coffee with several women I've never met?* I smiled, thinking of the experience at Olga's home in Russia decades before.

The next morning I showed up at Susan's home. It was sleeting, so we moved from the Turquoise Table inside to her dining room table. I wish I could bottle up the feeling of being included and welcomed that morning. I sat at the table with four women, friends for decades, drinking homemade peppermint lattes with gingerbread garnishes. And it was as if I had known them forever too.

It takes special hearts to welcome a complete stranger into the fold. At Susan's that morning I was the stranger who was very well loved. What an encouragement to pass it on.

The word *recipe* means both to give and to receive. It's a

beautiful paradox, the fullness of giving and receiving. Likewise, to experience its fullness, hospitality requires us to be both host and guest.

Sometimes we are the guest and sometimes we are the host. It's not either/or. It's both/and. Jesus models this in His ministry—relying on the hospitality of strangers, having no real home. Yet at the same time He teaches us how to be a host by His perfect example.

Easy No-Knead Bread

There's nothing better than freshly baked bread. But sometimes thinking about proofing the yeast, waiting for the dough to rise, and kneading can be overwhelming. This simple no-knead bread recipe rises magically overnight and bakes into a beautiful round loaf with a crunchy crust and soft center. My family loves this bread, and I love making it and sharing it! The recipe is so easy you can make two loaves at a time—one to enjoy and one to share with a friend or neighbor.

Share the bread. Share the love!

3 cups all-purpose flour

1 teaspoon quick rise, instant yeast

2 teaspoons salt

1 teaspoon sugar

1 $^1/_2$ cups water

In a large nonmetallic bowl stir together the flour, yeast, salt, and sugar. Add the water and stir with a wooden spoon until the dough comes together. The dough will be slightly sticky with a shaggy consistency. Cover the bowl with plastic wrap and place in a warm, draft-free spot overnight. Let dough rest 8 to 12 hours.

The next morning, with lightly floured hands, gently scoop the dough out of the bowl onto a floured surface. Form the dough into a round ball. Cover the dough with the plastic wrap or a tea towel and let rest 30 minutes to 1 hour while the oven preheats.

Preheat the oven to 450 degrees. Place a large (5- to 6-quart) enamel or cast-iron covered pot in the oven as it heats. When the oven finishes preheating, carefully remove the pot. Place the dough in the heated pot, cover, and bake for 30 minutes. Remove the lid and continue to bake the bread 10 minutes more, until golden brown.

Pumpkin and White Bean Soup

Every year we host a soup party on Halloween. The idea was born out of practicality when the children were little and had friends from school whose neighborhoods weren't as festive for trick-or-treating. In an effort to make sure all the kids had a safe and fun place to spend the evening, a tradition was born. We never know how many families to expect, and folks tend to drop in throughout the evening, so I make a couple different soups and keep them simmering on the stove.

- 1 tablespoon butter
- 1 onion, chopped
- 1 tablespoon fresh sage, chopped
- 6 cloves garlic, crushed
- 1/4 teaspoon crushed red pepper, more to taste
- 1/4 teaspoon cumin
- 2 1/2 cups vegetable broth
- 1 (15-oz.) can cannellini beans, rinsed and drained
- 1 (15-oz.) can pumpkin puree
- 1 cup milk

¾ teaspoon salt

2 tablespoons apple cider vinegar

In a saucepan, melt butter over medium-high heat. Add onion, sage, and garlic. Sauté until mixture is soft and fragrant. Add

crushed red pepper and cumin. Stir in ½ cup of the broth. Mix until well combined.

Pour the onion mixture into a large blender. Add remaining 2 cups of broth, beans, and pumpkin. Blend on high until smooth. You may have to blend in batches depending on the size of your blender.

Return puree to saucepan. Stir in milk and season with the salt. Bring to a simmer, cook 5 to 10 minutes, until warm. Stir in apple cider vinegar.

Serve warm with a dollop of Homemade Basil Pesto (see page 170) and Easy No-Knead Bread (see page 128).

Tips for Hosting a Neighborhood Soup Party

Variety. Make two pots of soup. Use recipes that serve a crowd or can be doubled easily.

Self-Serve from the Stove. Since our soup party is come and go, I leave the soup simmering on the stove and encourage guests to help themselves.

Use a Mix of Bowls and Mugs. Don't worry if you don't have enough bowls; pull out all your coffee mugs, too. It's fun to mix it up.

Set up a Topping Bar. Soup toppings are the best part! Put out plenty of versatile toppings such as cheese, chips, chives, and sour cream.

Make It a Potluck. Depending on the size of your gathering, why not make it a potluck? Ask your neighbors to bring a pot of their favorite soup.

Head to the Front Yard. We take our mismatched mugs of soup and head outside to greet neighbors and trick-or-treaters at the Turquoise Table.

The Broken Table

> We are all broken,
> that's how the light gets in.
>
> *Ernest Hemingway*

My friends and I were being interviewed for our local newspaper when the Turquoise Table suddenly gave way. Mid-conversation, the table's bench cracked under me. I shrieked, which, of course, cracked us up. We broke the table! Here's the best part. Not only was it during a photo shoot, but it also happened on the second anniversary of the day I put the table in my front yard.

Even though our initial conversation felt staged for the interview because we were aware of the camera's presence, the timing of the bench breaking turned out to be a silver lining. Nobody got hurt—it was just a slight jolt—but it served as the ultimate icebreaker.

One of the women exclaimed, "Don't put the picture of the broken table in the paper!"

"No!" I jumped in. "Make *sure* to put the picture of the broken table in the paper. This isn't a table for the perfect; this is a table for people with trials and flaws."

I told the photographer about the Turquoise Table. "It's when we come to the table, broken and vulnerable, not hiding behind our perfection, that the realness happens . . . when we're really human we connect."

The photographer had been an outsider, merely there to do his job, but this confession pulled him in. "This is really beautiful." He was engaged in our conversation. "I'm going to get a small turquoise table for my apartment balcony," he said.

After the photographer left, we propped the bench up with an upside-down clay pot and continued to sit around and visit, opening up the conversation to a whole new level. We recognized the metaphor: when we come to the table broken, deep friendships can happen. The only way we'll truly expand and deepen our relationships is through our vulnerability. Our morning continued with each of us gently laying broken pieces of our lives on the table—the fragile marriage, the volatile temper, the compulsion to shop, the binge on Fritos, the loss of trust in a child.

BROKEN LIVES, AUTHENTIC RELATIONSHIPS

Why is it so hard to admit our weaknesses? There is nothing better than the moment you hear a friend say something that resonates so deeply within you that you reach out with relief and say, "Thank you for sharing that . . . I thought I was the only one."

And it's more than just confessing superficial flaws—we all have laundry piled up, messy kitchens, and too many nights spent in the drive-thru line for "family dinner." It's the brokenness of our own humanity we find so shameful to share.

Best-selling author and psychologist Brené Brown teaches that vulnerability is a process, one that leads to compassion. It starts with acknowledging our own brokenness. In *I Thought It Was Just Me (But It Isn't)* Brown wrote,

> We are "those people." The truth is . . . we are the others. Most of us are one paycheck, one divorce, one drug-addicted kid, one mental health illness, one sexual assault, one drinking binge, one night of unprotected sex, or one affair away from being "those people"—the ones we don't trust, the ones we pity, the

ones we don't let our kids play with, the ones bad things happen to, the ones we don't want living next door.

There's a quote making the rounds on social media that says, "Instead of building a taller fence, we should build a longer table." We don't want "those people" living next door because their problems make us face our own. So we build fences, walls, or whatever proverbial barrier we need in order to hide. What we should be building is tables and inviting everyone to join us there.

Vulnerability requires honesty. Simple, right? If only it were

We spread more light into a dark world by opening our doors than hiding behind them.

that easy to be honest with our-selves about the true condition of our hearts. Yet we live in a culture that bombards us with a mirage of perfect—perfect Instagram feeds, perfect bodies, perfect jobs, perfect children, perfect marriages, perfect homes, perfect, perfect, perfect.

If perfection had a slogan, I think it would be something like: "Perfection, the preferred hiding place of people everywhere."

It's a lie.

Merriam-Webster defines *vulnerable* as "capable of being phys-ically or emotionally wounded; open to attack or damage."

> ## Truths to Remind Yourself of the Beauty of Brokenness
>
> - You are enough, even in—especially in—your imperfection.
> - Comparing yourself to others is a trap, rooted in the fear of inadequacy.
> - Peace comes with embracing who you are in this moment—not who you desire to be in the future.
> - Coming to the table is a step of faith that places a broken person side by side among new friends in the beauty of community.
> - Courage is contagious, and broken people build each other up—that's beautiful.
> - Love is always more powerful—and beautiful—than fear, and broken people love well.

Well, that's no fun! I'll take the surprise behind Door Number 2, please. Maybe it will be a lifetime supply of duct tape to hold all the pieces of my cracked, broken, messy self together. Vulnerability presents a paradox—the only way to wholeness is through our brokenness. In our weakness, we are strong.

Wounds don't heal by themselves. They require clean water, antibiotic ointment, fresh air, and a bandage. Deeper wounds require medical expertise. Our shattered, interior, broken bits are no different. We need people—free of judgment, but full of wisdom—and time. Healing happens in community with other people. And it starts at the table.

Brokenness is a perfectionist's worst enemy.

Anna Schell

The most beautiful people I know wear their imperfections with grace and confidence. It's not pride or false humility, but a self-assurance from well-earned battle scars. There's a reason we aren't attracted to "fake" or "shallow" people. Perfect is *boring*! Have you learned anything interesting from someone stuck perpetually in the trap of perfection? No, me neither. I leave feeling worse about myself. Our flaws and idiosyncrasies are what make us interesting to one another. Rather than let our differences define and divide us, we must celebrate them.

BREAKING UP WITH PERFECTION

For me, it's easy to free-fall into the perfection pit and allow the holiness of hospitality to revert to entertainment. Entertainment puts the emphasis on *me*. Does my house look okay? Gosh, I wish we had different kitchen cabinets. I should paint them. NOW. I hope I bought the right cheese for the appetizer tray. Do cheddar and grapes really go together? Maybe I should have splurged on blue cheese too. But it's so stinky. I should have gotten the blue cheese; stinky is good.

Pride prompts a spin cycle of worry. And it's an endless cycle because when entertainment is the goal, the house will never be ready. There will always be "one more thing" to do.

Hospitality takes the posture of humility, no longer seeking to impress but to serve. The heart of hospitality is to make people feel welcome and at ease. We can go through the motions to entertain, or we can adopt a way of life that opens us up—good, bad, and ugly—to others.

When we acknowledge and understand the places in our lives that are broken, there's less room for judgment of others. We're breaking patterns of perfectionism and letting things just be. That loss of judgment frees us from pride. In keeping things Pinterest perfect, we're entertaining everyone but fooling no one. Hospitality starts with our acknowledging our weaknesses, strengths, and shortcomings. That's

We strive for independence— we fight for it. But we were not meant to live as lone rangers.

how we empathize with others. Grace can only flow freely through cracked pots.

The first step toward authenticity can be as simple as acknowledging our deep need for one another. When my son, Will, was a toddler, he would be so proud of whatever task he had just accomplished—brushing his teeth, putting away a toy—he would exclaim with pride, "I can do it all *my byself.*" I loved the irony of his declaration and never brought myself to correct him. To this

day our family uses the phrase to mean, "I got it, I don't need any help."

Being in community means depending on other people. Our weaknesses reveal our dependency on God and others, which is countercultural in our society, the country that celebrates independence in the land of the free. We strive for independence—we fight for it. But we were not meant to live as lone rangers. We'd miss the opportunity for others to step in and fill the cracks. Belonging is an act of receiving and giving.

My friend Jenni and I had a conversation recently about how it's so much easier for us to give than receive. Whether it's receiving a gift or asking for help, we both acknowledged it's a challenge for us.

"Why is it so hard for women—or maybe it's just us—to receive help?" I really wanted to know.

"I feel like it's an imposition. Everyone is so busy," Jenni started. She shared that her neighbor recently stopped by and asked to borrow an egg. Of course Jenni was delighted to give her neighbor an egg. In fact, she said it made her feel good, nostalgic even.

"When we were growing up," Jenni said, "if Mom needed an egg she'd ask me to head across the street and get one from Miss Leah. I'd dash out the door, ask for an egg, thank my neighbor, and then scurry back across the front yard cupping the egg safely in my two hands. Why don't we do that anymore?"

Needing an egg doesn't reveal a vulnerability or expose our brokenness, but it's a great reminder that part of loving others

---

Ask a Neighbor for Help

Asking for help is hard to do. We tend to think of the "ask" as an imposition or burden. Most people, however, enjoy being asked for small favors. I know it makes me happy to think I've helped meet a need in an unexpected, unplanned way. See if asking for help leads to the opportunity to get to know a neighbor better.

Hopefully you'll get to return the favor sometime!

- Borrow a tool or lawn mower.
- Instead of dashing to the store, ask for an egg or cup of sugar.
- If you know your neighbor has a certain skill or expertise, ask for advice.
- Ask for assistance walking your pet or moving a piece of furniture.
- If you know your neighbor is headed on an errand, ask her to pick up milk or stamps.

---

is allowing them to love us too. When we practice asking for help in small ways, we come to believe we are not a burden but a blessing.

We will never be fully ready or prepared for brokenness. God will heal our broken hearts, but we must give Him all the pieces. He never promises to fix our hardships, but He does promise to be with us always, Emmanuel, even in—or especially in—our brokenness. And He gives us the gift of one another to work it out in community.

KEEPING IT REAL

I let the Turquoise Table sit broken for a month, maybe longer. Partially because it took a while for repairs to get to the top of my to-do list. Plus, it was still functional with the bench propped up on the upside-down clay pot. Truthfully, I needed the visual reminder of the broken table. The cracked wood and splintered bench was hard-earned—weathering the hot Texas summers and two years of carrying the emotional and physical weight of those who gathered. Eventually the wood had to be fixed, but I know the table is stronger and more beautiful having been broken. And so are we all.

Table Talk

We often kick off our mornings at the table with a round of "hold the bucket." Each person gets a turn to purge everything on her stress/worry/need list into a pretend bucket. Others in the group take turns holding the bucket and listening. Using the "hold the bucket" metaphor allows us to give verbal cues like "Time to pass the bucket" if one of us is being a table hog. Or "Girl, I'm holding the bucket" if another is bottling up and needs to share. Try holding the bucket for one another at your next Turquoise Table gathering. To my knowledge no one's ever kicked the bucket while holding one!

A Turquoise Table Story

After Carolyn suffered a significant and tragic loss, she needed time and space to process her grief on her own terms and away from social obligations. Inspired by her childhood garden in Mexico, Carolyn decided to create a healing garden around her Turquoise Table as a place to provide comfort and peace for herself, her family, and neighbors.

"I remember a lime blossom plant in our yard called *tilia* in Spanish," Carolyn said. "When I was sad, upset, or simply had a stomach ache, my mother would tear off a leaf, boil it, and make it into a soothing tea." Offering a simple but meaningful gift was something Carolyn wanted to pass on to others who might be in need of comfort.

Carolyn began her initiative by taking bundles of herbs from her garden to nearby neighbors, as well as leaving small bags of the various offerings out on her Turquoise Table. She added a sign inviting anyone passing by to take some.

"I love the sense of community the Turquoise Table represents, but I knew that I couldn't use mine for block parties or morning coffees," said Carolyn. "Those are happy events, and I struggle with sadness. Gardens are places of calm, and that is what I need in my life. I know there are plenty of others needing the same thing, so my Turquoise Table is a place of quiet retreat rather than social gathering."

Unfortunately, too often it was Carolyn's four-legged neighbors that got to the helpings first (her neighborhood has a vast population of wild deer), so her plan had to be modified. Now all of the herbs and flowers remain in the backyard behind the fence, but neighbors are welcome to walk back anytime. She also planted a whole new crop of herbs to make them multiply faster, and has plans to expand a side garden that will enable people to come and go even less conspicuously.

"My hope is that those experiencing sadness or difficulties come to the table and enjoy the garden," Carolyn said. "Smell the flowers, take herbs to use in a recipe, or make an herbal tea. They can sense a true connection without feeling pressured by face-to-face conversations that require smiling through the pain."

Additionally, she uses the table as a peaceful place to connect with her family. Enjoying a snack outside with her children enables them to unwind together and share the day's events.

"Being outside, in nature, is so peaceful. Sitting with my husband and children, few words are needed."

The Broken Table

Reaching out and caring for those around us can take on many forms, and not every table needs to be designated strictly for neighborhood socials. Quiet community is just as powerful. Carolyn is an inspiration for others to be Front Yard People in whatever way is most authentic for them.

Mint Simple Syrup

Mint is one of the most common and versatile herbs. Known for comforting upset tummies and relieving tension headaches, it's also one of the easiest herbs to grow. In many cultures mint symbolizes hospitality and is offered as a gesture to welcome friends and guests. In Spanish, mint is called yerba bueno, *or good herb.*

1 cup water

1 cup sugar

1 cup fresh mint leaves

In a small saucepan bring water and sugar to a boil over medium-high heat. Stir until sugar dissolves. Reduce heat and add mint leaves. Simmer for 2 minutes and remove from heat. Cool completely. Strain into a small glass container, pressing on the mint leaves to release the flavor. Store in refrigerator for 2 weeks.

Use mint simple syrup to sweeten ice tea or lemonade!

Hibiscus Mint Iced Tea

4 cups water

4 hibiscus tea bags

1/2–1 cup mint simple syrup, depending on how sweet you
like it

Ice cubes

In a large saucepan bring 4 cups of water to a boil. Remove from
heat and add 4 hibiscus tea bags. Steep for 15 minutes. Cool.

In a pitcher add 4 cups of hibiscus tea and 1 cup of mint
simple syrup. Stir and serve over ice.

9

EXTENDING THE TABLE

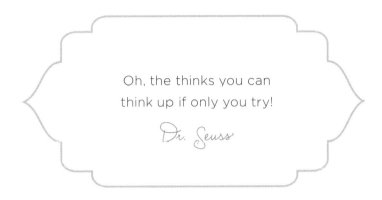

Oh, the thinks you can
think up if only you try!

Dr. Seuss

One day I noticed a mason jar with fresh-cut flowers sitting on the Turquoise Table. There was no note or explanation, just the delightful surprise of a small bouquet.

I called Mandy. "Did you leave a sweet bouquet of flowers on the Turquoise Table?"

"No, but I wish I had," she replied.

Maybe it was Amy? Not her either.

Surely then it was my mother. "Mia? Thank you for the mason jar and flowers you left on the Turquoise Table."

"What flowers?"

For the next few days, I continued to ask neighbors and friends about the flowers that appeared out of nowhere at the table. When no one fessed up, I decided the only possible explanation was that fairies exist and the Turquoise Table has its very own Flower Fairy.

The flower delivery wasn't a one-time thing, nor was it limited to my table. I learned the Flower Fairy enjoyed leaving flowers at other Turquoise Tables across town as well. Such a little gesture, but it kept spreading. To this day, the Flower Fairy continues to delight with surprise deliveries of blossoms and blooms—simple grocery store bouquets. Word spread like wildflowers, and tiny parcels of love have been left on Turquoise Tables near and far.

> It is only with the heart that one can see rightly. What is essential is invisible to the eye.
> *Antoine de Saint-Exupéry*

The Flower Fairy found a way to contribute to the Turquoise Table as an anonymous giver of joy. She represents a beautiful example of how each of us plays a role in community. I don't know the Flower Fairy's situation—maybe she doesn't have a front yard, or lives where a homeowners' association discourages picnic tables painted turquoise.

Here's what I do know about the Flower Fairy—she shows up. She contributes what she can and brings great joy to those of us with Turquoise Tables in our neighborhood. It's so simple, but this anonymous giver encourages me every time. It's like a secret nod of affirmation to keep gathering people, to keep loving them.

It takes each of us to make a difference for all of us. Look around—there is a special way for you to be part of your community. Maybe you are like the Flower Fairy. Maybe your role is not to be the one with the Turquoise Table but to encourage and support. Everyone has something to offer to make it all work together and function well. When one becomes many, each contributing the gifts they have been given, community is formed.

AN UNEXPECTED CONNECTION

The Flower Fairy isn't the only unexpected guest at the Turquoise Table. About a year after I first sat in my front yard at the table, I was invited to speak at a kickoff rally for the Love Where You Live neighborhood initiative in Austin. In the middle of my brief talk about my experience getting to know neighbors at the Turquoise Table, my phone vibrated in the back pocket of my jeans.

Thankfully the phone was on silent. I left the stage and looked at my messages to find a tweet from someone in the audience.

"We make picnic tables—let's talk."

One tweet led to another, and eventually I met the good folks at ReWork Project face-to-face. ReWork, a local nonprofit, employs men and women transitioning out of homelessness by training them in skills they can use in the marketplace. In a small warehouse in South Austin, several men had been making picnic tables, Adirondack chairs, birdhouses, and other woodworking projects. After getting to know each other, we decided a partnership was a no-brainer. Building Turquoise Tables gives men like Howard, Anthony, and Clifton the opportunity to stay employed and off the streets—not to mention covered head to toe in Nifty Turquoise paint.

> Do what you can, with what you have, where you are.
> *Teddy Roosevelt*

One of the first tables that ReWork made was for another local nonprofit in Austin, Ronald McDonald House Charities of Central Texas. A friend of the Ronald McDonald House donated the table to create a welcoming, safe place for families who are clearly in a time of crisis and stress. The Turquoise Table sits

EXTENDING THE TABLE

No front yard? No problem.

Shelly, who lives in England, found a creative way to be part of the Front Yard People community. "We don't have yards in London, so I painted my front door turquoise as a symbolic way to welcome to all who enter our home."

Mary Helen encountered opposition from her homeowners' association after she put a table in her front yard. She persisted, writing a letter explaining the purpose of the Turquoise Table is to encourage community and gathering. They finally granted her permission to keep gathering at the table.

Tim wasn't as successful with his HOA in Tennessee, which unfortunately forced the table into the backyard. "In spite of the opposition, we continue to live as Front Yard People and have weekly meals for our neighbors—about thirty people each week."

Stephanie has an unusually large front yard—she lives on a farm with her family in Arkansas. "We don't live in a neighborhood anymore. But we do have chickens, a fire pit, and a swimming pool. Our Turquoise Table is a reminder that we live with an open door to friends to drop by to play or stay!"

outside next to the playground under the happy grin of the iconic Ronald McDonald himself.

On a recent visit, Carolyn, the executive director of Ronald McDonald House Charities of Central Texas, shared the story of "the phone call" with me. Her office overlooks the Turquoise Table and playground. Carolyn noticed during one month, every afternoon at about 2:00 p.m., one of their guests—a mother of a chronically ill child—would sit at the Turquoise Table and make a phone call. Carolyn learned the mother was calling her husband, who was back home with their other children. Here in the middle of the day, like clockwork, they found the only time they'd both

have a break to catch up and connect. The mother would step outside even in cold weather and sit at the table to talk to her husband.

"I saw it and recognized the Turquoise Table was a place of respite and stability for this family with all the other chaos in their lives. I knew the table was a great idea. It was fun!" Carolyn said. "But when I saw the way this mother intuitively returned to the table, I realized its significance."

You don't have to provide the table in your front yard, but you can help get the table out into the neighborhood to places where people can find peace, community, and even a quiet place to connect.

CREATE PLACES TO GATHER WHERE YOU LIVE, WORK, AND PLAY

The Flower Fairy, ReWork Project, and the Ronald McDonald House donor each found a way to play a role in creating community around a Turquoise Table. The Flower Fairy had eyes to see that flowers, given anonymously, might bring joy. The folks at ReWork Project recognized their woodworking skills could be used to create multilayers of community with ongoing impact. The generous donor at the Ronald McDonald House had the heart to believe a picnic table might serve as a bright place of hope for families. In every instance, unexpected needs were met. That's what happens when we show up.

ACTIVITY

With your friends and neighbors, take a look at the Love Where You Live activity from chapter 3 and identify where people are gathering in your life and community. Try to create a communal table—pitch in together and donate a table to a school, a workplace, or the local park.

Creative Places for the Turquoise Table

- Community garden
- School playground
- Church courtyard
- Local coffee shop
- Retirement home
- Children's hospital waiting room
- Public library
- Common areas at office complex
- Apartment community space
- Neighborhood bus stop
- Farmer's market

When B. J. and two of her coworkers noticed a shady spot of grass outside their office window, they collaborated to put a Turquoise Table in the building's courtyard. "We realized we didn't know our business neighbors and wanted to change that," said B. J. The trio has organized campus-wide potluck lunches and used the table for client meetings. Recently they saw women gathered at the table while another played the flute for them. "It's remarkable how the table has brought us of our offices, and really, outside of ourselves."

THE TURQUOISE TABLE

In San Antonio, a group of teachers decided to use the Turquoise Table in a classroom setting. Each child got a chance to sit at the table and invite a different classmate to join him or her, to get to know new friends. The teachers created conversation cards for the children, prompting them to ask about a favorite pet or color.

Not one of these people made a complicated three-course meal or fretted over guest lists, money, or time. Yet in every instance hospitality was extended in life-giving ways.

A Turquoise Table Story

When the Good Earth Farm to Market opened in San Antonio, the organizers donated six Turquoise Tables to provide welcome spots for neighbors, friends, and visitors to gather. Opening day arrived with great fanfare, and I was there with my mother, Mia, and daughters, Anna, Ellie, and Sarah, to celebrate.

Tents transformed an ordinary parking lot with pop-up farm stands featuring an abundance of organic vegetables, fresh eggs, homemade tamales, and assortments of breads and baked goods. Two food trailers provided heartier fare for hungry shoppers. There was live music, a petting zoo for children, and sidewalks were turned into colorful canvases for chalk art. At the heart of this new and thriving community, people sat down to eat, drink coffee, and talk at the Turquoise Tables.

The mission of the Good Earth Farm to Market is to build community and bring health and life to the neighborhood. It was the first farmer's market in this part of San Antonio. Pamela, the lead organizer, saw the needs of the community and believed a farmer's market could bring health and vitality to the neighborhood while building community.

"We like to think of the Good Earth Farm to Market as an invitation for the whole neighborhood to our collective front yard every Saturday," Pamela said.

Mia, the girls, and I table-hopped, meeting new people in between shopping for fresh veggies and herbs and eating breakfast tacos. The people-watching was amazing. An older woman wearing a hat to shade her face from the sun enjoyed a moment to rest and relax at one of the Turquoise Tables. She was soon joined by a young family with a baby who was just learning to walk. The little girl wobbled down the picnic table holding on to the bench for support. The woman in the hat greeted the baby with a big grin and invited the family to join her at the table where a conversation ensued.

At another table a man covered in tattoos sat next to moms with children in strollers, enjoying conversations and breakfast tacos. A policeman leaned up against a table chatting with neighbors in a casual way. Each scene showcased how we're all welcome at the Turquoise Table.

I was struck by the simplicity of it all. Everyone played a role doing what comes naturally—farmers brought food, neighbors shopped and strolled, and everyone ate. They didn't have to plan something new or be different from who they are. The tattoo guy, the woman with her hat, the policeman, the parents with hungry children—it was a melting pot of what community looks like when you come as you are.

Pamela's vision was realized. And the Turquoise Table was extended to the Good Earth Farm to Market as an invitation for the neighborhood to live together as Front Yard People.

Homemade Basil Pesto

Bring home a basket of basil from your local farmer's market and whip together a classic pesto. The best thing about pesto is it's simple, delicious, and tastes good with just about everything. Toss it with your favorite pasta, spread it on bread or crackers for an easy appetizer, or add a dollop to scrambled eggs for a flavorful twist to your morning routine.

> **2 cups fresh basil leaves**
>
> **1/2 cup freshly grated Parmesan cheese**
>
> **1/3 cup pine nuts**
>
> **2 garlic cloves, rough chopped**
>
> **1/2 cup olive oil**
>
> **Salt and black pepper to taste**

In a food processor, add basil, cheese, pine nuts, and garlic. Pulse several times until ingredients are chopped. With the processor running, slowly add the olive oil in a steady stream. You may need to scrape down the sides. Blend until pesto is thick and fully combined.

Want to change things up? Using the same directions, try one of these pesto combos:

Pumpkin seeds and cilantro

Walnuts and arugula

Pistachio and spinach

Almonds and sun-dried tomatoes

10

A Table for All Seasons

There is a time for everything,
and a season for every activity
under the heavens.

Ecclesiastes 3:1 NIV

One spring afternoon our daughter Sarah and I decided to sit at the table, only to discover it was covered in bird poop. Sarah, then seven years old, was completely grossed out. Before we could enjoy time at the table, we needed to roll up our sleeves and clean. We headed to the garage, grabbed a bucket of water and dish soap, and got busy scrubbing.

Sarah and I made light of the poop, cracking jokes and splashing each other with the soapy water. I'm all about finding silver linings and, believe it or not, even bird poop can make for a great teaching moment. We have to take care of the things that are important in our lives.

"But, Mom, it's just a picnic table."

"Yes, but the Turquoise Table is where we enjoy time together with our family and friends. We eat here, talk here, play here. No one wants to sit at a table covered in bird poop!"

"I guess the birds really feel at home here too!"

Sarah scrubbed a little harder, proud of her contribution to taking care of the table where so much activity and life take place.

While I had Sarah's attention, I continued to teach my daughter lessons I had learned at the various tables in my life. I learned to clear dishes after supper from my mother. In France, I learned to sweep bread crumbs from the tablecloth with a funny tool that looked like a toothbrush married to a knife. While there, I also learned to cook and serve simple meals, even though I didn't speak the language well. In Russia, I learned to be polite and eat fish head soup without gagging and offending my host. I didn't eat the eyes, though. Sometime there are limits on just how polite you can be.

> Life keeps us all running in a thousand directions. I want my kids to know how to stop, connect, and have a real conversation with me. And through our Turquoise Table, my family is able to gather and really unplug.

Tending the table matters. It's not as fun to clean bird poop as it is to host a lemonade stand, but being prepared and taking care of the table without grumbling is an important part of offering hospitality to others.

The Turquoise Table

Despite the cleaning and preparation and tending, the time came for a new table. Even Turquoise Tables have a season. After the Turquoise Table cracked during the photo shoot, I asked my friends at ReWork to help me repair the bench. Although Anthony, Clifton, and Howard did a first-rate job on the repairs, I knew it was only a matter of time before the old wood table would need replacing.

At first I resisted. I didn't want to get rid of the original table—so much had happened there. Mia joked, as only a mother could, that I should send it to the Smithsonian. It probably wasn't that important to the American public, but the Turquoise Table was important to me. I wanted to hold on; it's hard to let go of things that matter deeply.

Season after season, the Turquoise Table had stood strong, a simple structure of wood, nails, and paint. The table had held hearts, guarded confessions, seen reconciliation, boosted dreams, collected tears, lifted prayers, heard stories, sealed friendships, strengthened community, and anchored me in faith and place. It felt bittersweet, if not altogether wrong, to get a new table.

SEASONS CALL FOR CHANGE

The morning ReWork delivered the new Turquoise Table wasn't at all what I expected. I imagined emotion and fanfare to commemorate the changing-of-the-guard moment. Scott, a ReWork volunteer, and Anthony, who builds tables, pulled up in a pickup truck with the new table. I caught up with Anthony, and in his quiet, slow voice he filled me in on the other guys at ReWork.

"Did you build this table?" I asked Anthony.

"No, I'm not building Turquoise Tables anymore," he replied.

"What? They must have given you a promotion!"

"Yes, I'm writing now. Starting my own blog, and will be writing for ReWork soon too," he said with humility.

For four years the staff and volunteers at ReWork have poured into men like Anthony, training them for far better lives than they ever dreamed possible when they were homeless on the streets. I was so proud of Anthony I couldn't stand it. He told me he guessed he'd built, or helped build, about fifty Turquoise Tables at ReWork. And now he has a new way to contribute, sharing his hard-earned words.

About that time, Elizabeth walked by with Clyde. I asked her what she thought we should do with the original Turquoise

> For years the staff and volunteers at ReWork have poured into men like Anthony, training them for far better lives than they ever dreamed possible when they were homeless on the streets.

Table. She suggested putting it in the side yard, facing the cul-de-sac, until we came up with a plan. Scott and Anthony offered to move the old table to the spot Elizabeth suggested. Then she said she liked the idea of donating the table. Inspired by Anthony and his successes, she thought maybe we could share the table so homeless men and women on the streets could use it. Other neighbors have chimed in too. We have so many ideas we're still deciding.

Anthony and Elizabeth reminded me that morning the Turquoise Table has never been the hero of this story. The heroes of this story are the people. It's always about the people who come to the table.

C. S. Lewis wrote in the Chronicles of Narnia, "Isn't it funny how day by day nothing changes, but when you look back everything is different." I can totally relate to Prince Caspian's sentiments.

Our children are growing up before our very eyes at this table. Lemonade stands have morphed into a gathering spot for teenagers. One of the girls' friends suggested the Turquoise Table needs a geofilter for Snapchat—whatever that means. Recently I looked out the kitchen window and got teary-eyed seeing the seven or eight cars parked by the table—cars driven by Will's friends who will soon graduate from high school.

A Table for All Seasons

LIVING IN THE MOMENT

Life at the Turquoise Table isn't one planned event after another. That pattern would revert our *being* back to *doing*, which leaves us depleted. Life at the Turquoise Table is a multitude of tiny moments, mini-miracles really, strung together like radiant beams of light over the places we call home.

Like the night my neighbor Monique reached out. I was at the kitchen sink doing dishes after dinner when she sent a text asking if we could talk. "Sure," I replied. "Meet me at the table in 5?" Monique had just made a major career decision and her mind was playing the second-guessing game. She didn't need advice— just someone to listen. Plus, we were both happy to escape briefly from the post-dinner family chaos. A few minutes into our chat, our eighty-year-old neighbor, Bob, drove by in his red Volkswagen convertible. If every neighborhood were blessed with couples like Peg and Bob Gerrie, the world would be a better place. Bob, whom we affectionately call the Mayor, asked how long Monique and I would be sitting at the table. Then he drove off, resembling Santa Claus with a mischievous twinkle in his eye, hollering, "Wait right there!"

Ten minutes later, Bob returned with warm sugar cookies—his favorite from McDonald's. He gave us the cookies in exchange for hugs and told us we were wonderful neighbors. As I hugged Bob, said good night to Monique, and headed back inside, I noticed the dish towel was still flung across my shoulder.

Then there's the coyote story. One morning news of an unusually large coyote seen on our street traveled fast via texts and social media. It occurred to me that Ned and Martha, who don't text or use Facebook, wouldn't know about the coyote who might still be lurking. I headed across the street to give them a heads-up and ended up sitting at their kitchen table for over an hour. We visited about happenings in the neighborhood, I filled them in

Celebrations at the Turquoise Table

There is always a reason, no matter the season, to bring people to the table. These are just a few of the creative ways our neighbors have celebrated at the Turquoise Table. You don't have to do all these, but hopefully this list will help get the creative juices flowing for year-round memories and love at the table.

- Valentine's Day: Place a basket of chocolate kisses on the table for a sweet treat.
- Easter: Host an egg-dyeing party.
- Mother's Day: Give a Turquoise Table to your mom.
- Father's Day: Grill dad a steak and enjoy supper at the Turquoise Table.
- Fourth of July: Create a watermelon bar; start a neighborhood parade.
- S'mores Day (August 10th!)
- Back-to-School
- Halloween: Host a neighborhood soup party before trick-or-treating.
- Thanksgiving: Host a "friendsgiving potluck feast."
- St. Nicholas Day: Celebrate the traditional saint's day by leaving chocolate coins and oranges on the door-steps of homes with young children.

ACTIVITY

Write a letter to your future self in whatever you imagine your next season of life to be. What do future seasons look like at your Turquoise Table? Who is there? What do those relationships look like? What can you do now to tend to the table to prepare for this hope or scene?

on our children's activities, and Ned told the story about building their house in the 1960s when our street still ended at the top of our hill.

As I listened to Ned's familiar story, noticing Martha in her housecoat, I thought of Ludmilla and her kitchen table thousands of miles away in Prague. I was having a Ludmilla moment right there at my neighbor's kitchen table while helping myself to more cream from the fridge for a second cup of coffee.

Ludmilla taught me to see what was in front of me all along. Ordinary people, brought together by proximity, all learning to belong to one another.

Of course, moments like these don't happen all at once or overnight. And everyone will have different experiences in the way community is shaped and strengthened. But the only way to find out is to begin.

A Turquoise Table Story

I heard my home phone ring, but couldn't find the receiver. We never use our landline anymore. The calls are automated anyway—from the pharmacy reminding us to pick up a prescription or a prerecorded political message.

I felt a familiar nudge, the one that moves me into action. This time it prompted me to listen to the message from my elderly neighbor, Doris, across the street.

"Kristin," her voice message began, "I felt a nudge in church to call you. The story our pastor shared about your Turquoise Table really spoke to me, and I just wanted to run an idea by you. Please call."

Hmmm . . . two nudges must mean something, I thought. I dialed her number.

Doris and I chatted about our neighborhood. She's lived here a long time, and as she was reminiscing about life on our street I imagined her children, who are now middle-aged like me, running barefoot through the grass in my front yard where my daughter's pink bicycle now stands propped up against the old oak tree firmly planted through it all.

"I just don't know my neighbors anymore," she confided. "And it makes me sad. We used to all know each other."

Doris continued, "What if we were to have a coffee? Do you think the neighbors would come?" She shared her idea—the one that had been nudging her since church.

"I think a coffee would be a fabulous idea, Doris! Yes, I think people would come. May I help you plan it?"

"That would be wonderful. I can bring scones or cookies," Doris offered.

We hung up the phone, and I called Mandy. I shared Doris's idea, and we sprang into action. Every neighborhood should have a saint like Mandy who organizes gatherings and keeps us all connected. We opted for a mid-morning coffee, knowing many of the women on our street were retired and home during the day. Mandy created the invitations, and two weeks before our coffee date I hand-delivered them to the thirty-four houses on our immediate street.

The morning I delivered the invitations I intended to ring each doorbell and hoped I would have a quick opportunity to extend the invitation to the coffee in person. I spent thirty minutes in Georgi's cozy living room home talking and twenty minutes chatting in Peg's kitchen. They were excited about the coffee and grateful Doris had the idea. I admit I had to stop ringing doorbells in order to make it to carpool on time. But as I quickly and quietly slipped invitations in mailboxes, I prayed.

> Lord, bring us together. Start something fresh and anew for Your glory. Right here in our neighborhood. On this very street. Knit us together. Remind us of the value of community.

Sixteen women came.

For two and a half hours conversation flowed. We ate sand tarts and old-fashioned pound cake and talked about matters big and small.

I paused and imagined God with great big beautiful eyes looking straight into my kitchen and smiling as we talked about family, the neighborhood, and our need for one another.

We have planned more coffees, and each of the women volunteered to host. Manju offered to teach us to cook in her kitchen using authentic curry and spices from India. Betty offered to host a happy hour so that we might expand our circle to working women. Kay sent a handwritten thank-you note and said her home was open anytime for the neighbors.

Doris's Sand Tarts

*My neighbor Doris is a wonderful cook who drops off baked goods
frequently for our family to enjoy. She brought these delicious sand tart
cookies to our neighborhood's first multigenerational coffee. Not only a
classic recipe passed on from decades ago, these cookies are multicultural as
well. In Mexico, the same recipe is called Wedding Cookies, and in Russia,
they are served with tea as Snowballs. Butter, sugar, and vanilla may be the
universal love language.*

1 cup (2 sticks) butter, softened

1 1/2 cups powdered sugar, divided

1 teaspoon vanilla extract

1 3/4 cups all-purpose flour

1 cup finely chopped pecans

Preheat oven to 300 degrees. Line 2 cookie sheets with
parchment paper.

With an electric mixer, cream the butter and 1/2 cup of the
powdered sugar until light and fluffy. Add the vanilla. Slowly add

the flour a little at a time and beat on low speed until combined and dough is formed. Stir in the pecans until well combined.

Roll dough into 1-inch balls and line on the parchment paper. Bake for 30 minutes or until golden brown.

While the cookies are still warm, roll in a bowl of remaining powdered sugar to coat. Return to cookie sheet to cool. Sprinkle any remaining powdered sugar on top of the sand tarts.

Old-Fashioned Almond Sheet Cake

Recently our neighbor Robert set up a care calendar to deliver meals to our older neighbors. Robert calls us the Neighborhood Care Angels. His organized spreadsheet lined me up with a homebound neighbor two streets over whom I had never met. I made a mental note of the delivery date, but promptly forgot! Hospitality is rarely convenient.

Thankfully, something nudged me to peek at the calendar a few hours before my scheduled delivery time. I keep a few containers of frozen soup on hand for moments like this, and I had a small loaf of cornbread, too. Sarah and I decided we had just enough time to make our new friend something sweet to round out the meal.

I've combined two of my favorite sheet cake recipes into a new favorite. One recipe comes from my grandmother and the other from my dear friend Jamie. The cake whips up in a hurry and is perfect to take to larger gatherings or cut in squares to deliver to several neighbors. You should have seen the smile on Mr. Langford's face when we shared a bite of almond sheet cake with him.

For the cake:

2 cups all-purpose flour*

2 cups sugar

1 teaspoon baking soda

1 teaspoon salt

1 cup butter (2 sticks)

1 cup water

2 eggs, slightly beaten

$1/2$ cup sour cream

1 teaspoon almond extract

For the icing:

4 cups powdered sugar

$1/2$ cup butter (1 stick)

$1/3$ cup milk

$1/2$ teaspoon almond extract

Preheat oven to 375 degrees. Generously grease a 12 x 17-inch rimmed baking sheet.

In a large mixing bowl combine flour, sugar, salt, and baking soda. Set aside.

In a medium saucepan, over medium-high heat, melt butter and water. Stir until fully combined. Pour melted butter into the flour mixture and mix well with an electric mixer.

Add eggs, sour cream, and almond extract. Continue mixing until batter is smooth.

Pour batter into prepared baking sheet. Bake for 18 to 20 minutes, until cake is just golden brown and set in the middle.

Cool cake completely before icing.

In the saucepan, melt butter over medium-high heat. Remove from heat and add milk and almond extract. Stir until combined.

In a large mixing bowl, mix powdered sugar and melted butter until icing is light and fluffy.

Spread icing evenly over the cake. Cut into squares and serve. At larger gatherings I serve this cake straight from the pan, just like my grandmother did.

*Jamie makes this cake with gluten free flour and it's just as delicious.

Front Yard People

FRONT YARD

Love invites us to move outside
into the neighborhood.

The day the Turquoise Table went missing, my phone was flooded with texts from concerned friends. We were out of town for the Fourth of July holiday, and our neighbors knew we weren't home to see that the table had mysteriously disappeared.

"You've been robbed!"

"Pranksters have done something with the Turquoise Table!"

One friend even texted me a photo of the exact spot where the table normally sits. The Turquoise Table has become part of the landscape in our neighborhood, a symbol of people belonging. Naturally, they were concerned. What my friends and neighbors didn't know was it was in good hands. Shannon had arranged for the table to be part of the neighborhood's Fourth of July parade. The Turquoise Table was safe and sound on a flatbed truck two blocks away.

I had nothing to do with the idea or planning for the parade. My neighbors made the fun happen, creating an entire Front Yard People theme for the float. Over the next three days, friends sent pictures and posted Facebook status updates documenting the progress as the float came together. Being away gave me perspective to see Front Yard People in action.

The float represented years of memories, trust, laughter, tears, and investment in each other's lives. All the small moments of gathering in simple ways manifested themselves as our neighbors rode as Front Yard People on a red, white, and turquoise float in the parade. We did it! And we're still doing it!

OPENING OUR LIVES AND HOMES TO OTHERS

In the beginning, the day the unpainted picnic table arrived at our house, I posed a hypothesis: What if we were to take all of our backyard activities—our birthday parties, bubble blowing, messy art activities, barbecue suppers—and simply move them to the front yard?

What would life look like if we lived as Front Yard People?

Try It

Take a look at the backyard activities you listed in chapter 2. You already have simple ways to begin living as Front Yard People. Pick one of your everyday activities and give it a go in the front yard at your Turquoise Table.

I had a hunch, but not a plan. There was no Front Yard People strategy, no 10-point Turquoise Table action plan, or hokey "Howdy, Neighbor" schedule. Heck, I didn't really even think about it.

Everyone asks me about the first day, the very first moment at the Turquoise Table. It's one of my favorite stories to tell—how Susan showed up just a few minutes after I sat at the table. But as much as I love that story and Susan, it is not the most significant moment. The defining moment happened long before the Turquoise Table was even a twinkle in my eye. It was the moment of surrender in the middle of the conference at the Austin Music Hall. When I was so desperate to hear from God with a plan, I begged Him to "SHOW ME! Show me what hospitality looks like to You. Show me how to love others in real community."

I was broken. I cried out for help. God showed up.

It's still the same today. Although gratefully not as dramatic. While there is no one-size-fits-all formula for life at the Turquoise Table, in my experience, there is a pattern: Notice the needs of others. Pray. Show up. Love.

Notice. Pray. Show up. Love.

Absolutely, there are days when it's blazing hot outside or I am tired, but showing up—even fifteen minutes at a time—matters. Love adds up. Love spreads. Love builds community.

Of course, community was always there, ours for the taking. We simply needed a nudge, a new way to see through the busyness and distractions in life. A place to slow down, sit down, and be present.

The Turquoise Table is that place. By design, picnic tables are not a place to sit alone; they invite community, especially when you gather out front, where everyone can see. It's a place where all people belong, and belonging is the ultimate gift of community.

These days, in addition to hanging out at my own Turquoise Table, I've become the holder of stories. Stories from people around the globe who have made the pledge to live as Front Yard People. Every week I hear from people who are beginning their adventures

Lessons from the Turquoise Table

In no particular order, here are highlights of the many lessons I continue to learn on the Front Yard People adventure:

- There isn't a *perfect* time to get a Turquoise Table, so I'm an advocate of *now.*
- When we are too busy to experience the relationships around us, we can end up feeling isolated and lonely.
- Spontaneous gatherings are just as important as planned ones—not to mention easier!
- We don't need permission to go outside and love. (For a copy of original permission slip, check out Matthew 22:37–39.)
- Having a buddy makes kicking things off easier and more fun.
- Going deep into community takes time; weather the seasons.
- Good things happen when we slow down and pay attention to the needs of those around us.
- The ministry of presence is something worth praying for every day.
- The greatest way God can work in our lives is through community.
- Love and hospitality are always intertwined.
- God invites us to the table. When we show up, He provides everything we need to extend the same invitation to others.

at the Turquoise Table. Some need affirmation—a last permission slip to "go for it!" Others want to work through a stumbling block that once shared doesn't seem so stumbly after all. Still others reach out who are in a difficult season, and despite wanting to have a Turquoise Table, it's just not possible. That's when sharing stories with one another—like the Flower Fairy or the farmer's market—helps illustrate there is always an unexpected way to connect with the people around you.

A TABLE FOR EVERYONE

Every time someone sends me a note or shares a photo of their Turquoise Table, my jaw drops and my heart flutters. *Whodda thunk?* I say it every time. Not out loud, though. Because I'm always truly dumfounded. Never in my wildest dreams could I have imagined Turquoise Tables multiplying like rabbits.

But then I remember the need: people are hungry for connection and a place to belong. And the truth—we were created to be in community by a God who loves us extravagantly. He loves all of us, each and every one. In order for us to even get a glimpse of what that kind of majestic love looks and feels like, we have to experience it through connection with others. So God gave us one another.

Today there are Turquoise Tables in nearly every state from California to Maine and five countries. I receive love notes from Nebraska and North Carolina, Africa and Australia, from tiny towns and urban centers. All over the world people are gathering at Turquoise Tables in all kinds of front yards and even on Main Street! We crave community—authentic connection to do our one-and-only crazy lives together. And what's better than living it out with the people right where you live, inviting them to your own front yard?

Will you join us? Your journey of loving your neighbors, creating a simple place for community, and daring to live as Front Yard People can begin now.

Front Yard People are the ones who raise their hands and say, "I'm all in!" Let's be people who build our lives around each other, opening our lives and homes to others, one Turquoise Table at a time.

ACKNOWLEDGMENTS

Thank you!

When you write a book on community, family, friends, and neighbors, it goes without saying that you could fill the pages of an additional book with nothing but love and thanks for the village that made it possible. The Turquoise Table is a collective effort, and it's a privilege to share the stories of very real people. Front Yard People isn't just a clever hashtag—Front Yard People are the men, women, and children who live across the street, in the cul-de-sac, up the hill, and around the corner.

My neighbors, the very first Front Yard People: You model what it means to open up your life and your home to others. Witnessing the way each of you expresses love is true joy! Thank you for trusting me to tell our story.

Tony: I did it. I finally finished a project I started. Thank you for believing in me and encouraging me to keep on going. I'm grateful for the truth you speak in my life, your wisdom on all things, your annoyingly reliable memory, and most of all your undying love and loyalty to our family. You are my most favorite person in the world, except on Tuesdays. I love you.

Will, Anna, Ellie, and Sarah: Thank you for being my people. I hope someday you'll appreciate the role you played in the story of the Turquoise Table. Your lemonade stands, cookie sales, outdoor projects, and even the embarrassing poses for Instagram serve as encouragement to me and so many others. I'm proud to be your mother and I love each of you more than you will ever know. Yes, even more than turquoise.

Mia and Popa: You set the larger table and taught me everything I know about family and the importance of loving others. The seeds of this book were planted long ago in a yellow kitchen on Park Lane. All those years of watching your tireless efforts to "build a better community" rubbed off! Let's be grateful God gave me a table and not a campaign. I love you both so much.

Jan: Where do I even begin? Thank you for teaching me God's word at Lamplighters, for modeling biblical hospitality, and always pointing me to Christ. Oh, and for being the best gift giver ever—the Blackberry Farm Bacon Jam is at the top of the countless treats you've given. But your friendship is the most priceless. I love you.

Our church community at Covenant Presbyterian: for praying, encouraging, and modeling what it looks like to follow Jesus wherever we live, work, and pray.

Thank you, Tricia, for introducing me to Janet Grant. Janet, you are so much more than an agent. You have been a mentor, counselor, and advocate for this story since our first conversation. I'm so grateful for your patience and incredible wisdom. What an adventure!

Ann: You deserve more than an acknowledgment. There are jewels in a special crown awaiting you. Quite simply, this book and ministry would not have moved forward without you. Your coaching, counsel, editing, wisdom, servant heart, and friendship are an answered prayer and the best gift. I might even share the Blackberry Farm Bacon Jam with you.

The wonderful team at HarperCollins Christian Publishing: Thank you for believing in the gift of the Turquoise Table and bringing our story to life. It's an honor to work with you.

For those of you who have held my hand, chatted on the phone, texted, voxed, run carpool, brought dinner, emailed, and prayed, thanks for being in my village: Kimberley, Julie, Jamie, Emily, Amanda, Isela, Erin, Claire, Mandy, Amy, Shannon, MaryBeth,

Lisa, Sue, Nicole, Cathy, Mindy, Holly, Lauren, Heather, Katelyn, Beth, Ashley, Wendy, Jenni, Christy, Lulu, Liz, Susie, Susan, Sandra, TeriLynne, Brooke, Stacy, the Frio PW Sisters, the Bible Babes, Lamplighters, and to the countless others who live far and wide and yet support me and the work of the Turquoise Table.

The focus groups at GSD&M and our neighborhood who read first drafts of the story and provided insights and wisdom to move the project forward. Thank you. The work is richer for your participation.

Bruce and Sanders: For painting the very first Turquoise Table. Your fingerprints are all over this story. I'm grateful.

For Harold, Anthony, Clifton, Allison, and Jacob at ReWork Project: I'll forever be grateful for the tweet that started our partnership. Thank you for helping us paint Austin turquoise. More importantly for the way you disciple, love, and build lives for our homeless community.

Christ Together Greater Austin: You love our city well. Thank you for producing the story of the Turquoise Table as part of the Love Where You Live initiative.

Deidox Films: Brent & Dave, thank you for capturing the divine story of Ludmilla. How we all came to meet and do life together is a chapter (or two!) for another book. Thank you Suzanne for being a link in the chain.

ACKNOWLEDGMENTS

For the faithful blog readers: You've supported, cheered, encouraged, and followed my musings through as many URL changes as hairstyles! Every comment, e-mail, and tweet came at just the right moment. Thank you.

Front Yard People: You amaze me! Many of your stories are told in this book. But, there are so many Turquoise Table stories I will never hear this side of heaven. Thank you for believing that when ordinary people gather at an ordinary picnic table extraordinary things will happen. Neighborhoods, communities, and lives are changing because of your availability and presence in your front yard.

ABOUT THE AUTHOR

Kristin Schell is an established speaker and blogger on the subjects of food, faith, and hospitality. Passionate about community, she has served at every level, from grassroots-level work in church and local nonprofits as well our nation's capital. As founder of the Turquoise Table and Front Yard People movement, Kristin travels the country speaking at conferences and events with an encouraging word on how to open our lives and homes to others. She lives in Austin, Texas, with her husband, Tony, and their four children.

For more information on the Turquoise Table please join Kristin at www.theturquoisetable.com

Turquoise Table Notes

Turquoise Table Notes

Turquoise Table Notes

Turquoise Table Notes